UNSTOPPABLE!

Surviving Is Just the Beginning.

**A True Tale of Lessons
Learned at Knife Point
And Other Crises, Peaks & Plateaus.
A Personal Commitment To
Not Only Survive, But
*To Thrive!***

By

GIGI STETLER

Published in 2009 by
JAS Literary Publishing
Fort Lauderdale, Florida
www.JASLiteraryPublishing.com

Printed in the United States of America

Names of some of the individuals in this book have been modified to protect privacy.

ISBN 10: 0-615-40507-X

ISBN 13: 978-0-615-40507-0

This book is available at quantity discounts for bulk purchases.

For information, call 1-888-587-3337 or visit www.2BeUNSTOPPABLE.com

CONTENTS

UNSTOPPABLE

The Story About A Girl Who Wouldn't Give Up

By Gigi Stetler

This book is dedicated to the joy of my life, my son Jarryd.

Introduction

As I look back on my personal and professional history, I find strength and joy in what I have accomplished, and fear and uncertainty in what lies ahead.

Over the past 22 years, I found myself working twice as hard to obtain half as much, being the only woman among the fat cat good old boys industry who told me to go home and bake cookies. Instead, I chose to stay at the office building an empire while I paid someone to bake cookies for me.

I will not accept defeat, nor will I waver; not after what I have been through. If I can survive being stabbed 21 times and left for dead, then I can certainly navigate through the cesspool of life and come out clean and smelling like a rose on the other end.

Throughout my tumultuous journey, I have learned that it's not how many times you are knocked down, but how many times you get up that count. I have been knocked off my horse more times than I can remember and the only thing separating success from failure, as I see it, it's the ability to get back up and start all over again.

I hope that my story will inspire you to achieve greatness in everything that you do and never accept defeat.

Chapter 1: Prologue
SURVIVING IS JUST THE BEGINNING

The *sensation* of running in a deep, heavy, wet fog is a surreal experience, to say the least. You know your feet are moving forward at a very animated pace, and you can *feel* them heading towards the ground with each step, just inches away, but you never actually see your feet touch the ground.

The fog is too thick for you to even see the ground, much less watch your feet reach it. And you just have to take it for granted that the ground is there, and that your feet will in fact meet the earth!

But, before you can think about what's going on and try to figure it out, you get caught up in the motion of the next step, and the one after that, and after that, and you're charging forward in the gray, wet void. But you don't really know where you're heading. Or, why!

At least, that's what I felt like, as loud, piercing screams startled me from my personal fog to return me back to reality.

I had been running in that deep, heavy *wetness* for a very long time, but I didn't seem to ever make any progress. In fact, I wasn't moving forward at all. I was just running, and running, and running. Once I realized I was motionless, I tried to lift my arms and legs. But they felt like lead, and I couldn't move them. I couldn't even open my eyes!

The loud screams jarred me out of my state of frozen consciousness. The sounds were jolting, loud, but *were they real*? I couldn't tell. After all, just seconds before, I had been totally oblivious to everything and anything, and now, I was hearing those piercing screams!

I don't know if I was awake, or not, but I *was conscious.* While my arms and legs still felt like lead, I turned my attention to opening my eyes. The more I wrestled with that task, the more conscious I became.

Suddenly, I realized the screams were coming from me!

As I fought to open my eyes, I *was able* to force a squint. That controlled the amount of light coming in, and cut down on the pain caused by the sharp brightness. Gradually things began to come into focus and, once they did, I looked around.

I was so caught up in absorbing where I was, I hadn't realized I was still screaming.

Moments later, a nurse came running in. Two more nurses immediately followed, each one heading to a different side of my hospital bed as they moved to render assistance. The first nurse went to the IV line running down an aluminum pole, from a saline bag hanging near the top from a short extended arm. The nurse inserted the needle-end of a hypodermic into a *'joint'* connector patched into the IV line, and began to push Demerol into the line to ease my physical pain.

That pain was the source of my screaming. It had been so intense that it pulled me out of the coma my body had retreated to, following 'the attack', as a way of dealing with the profound hurting, the mental shock and the sheer emotional trauma of it all.

While the initial danger had passed, the coma gave way to a semi-conscious state of oblivion. There was still great discomfort, from multiple stab wounds, and, in addition to crying out when a sharp jolt tore through me, I was also yelling. *"Make him stop! Make him stop!"*

The nurse on the right side spoke to me in calm, soothing voice, as she rested her right hand on my forearm and stroked my hair with her left hand. The warmth of her touch reassured me and eased some of the tension from the agitated state I was in.

"You were only dreaming, Gigi. You're safe now. The nightmare is over, and the man who attacked you is in jail," the nurse said.

"He can't hurt you anymore. Rest now, and let your body get stronger. Go back to sleep. There will be time to talk later."

When I awakened hours later, I was told I was in the Trauma Center at Mt. Sinai Hospital on Miami Beach. Lying in that hospital bed, I reflected not only on the days in my immediate past, but my overall past. Perhaps shaped by the most recent events, my mood was grim. And the future didn't look any better!

Early the next morning as the morning sun broke through the blinds, *reality entered* the room, long before a nurse ever pushed open the hospital room door, to check on me and ask me about my breakfast order.

Around dawn, when I first began to come out of the light fog which accompanied my restlessness through the night, between being asleep and awake, I had started to remember the events which put me in that room.

I was now in a hospital with more than 200 stitches because a crazy bastard by the name of *Jose Perro* went insane and used me as his piñata. But he didn't hit me with a stick. He stabbed me repeatedly. I was in my apartment, waiting for the 911 operator to come on the line, when Jose stormed through the door, charged at me and struck me in the chest.

As I fell to the floor, I wondered what the hell had just happened. As soon as I hit the tiles, I saw a deep-red stream of blood flowing out of the spot on my chest where he punched me. It all seemed so bizarre and I found myself floating in a sea of surreal denial. This can't be happening. Then, I saw a crazed look in Jose's eyes and a seven-inch fishing knife in his right hand. If this *isn't real,* I want to wake up *right now!*

4

He struck me again. And again. And then again. Sheer panic took me over completely as I saw his hand pulling back and plunging forward, again and again.

I tried to defend myself by grabbing the wet blade, fighting to keep it from reaching my chest again, but I had no strength. The knife cut deeply into my hand as that bastard continued stabbing me. I was fighting for my life... and losing.

I heard the faint voice of the 911 operator from the receiver on the table, where I dropped it when Perro lunged at me the first time.

"Hello? Can you hear me?" the operator asked. *"What's going on, in there? Do you need assistance?"*

I couldn't respond. And I couldn't reach the phone. Perro kept telling me he loved me as he continued to stab me, over and over, trying to reach my heart. In self-defense, I grabbed at the knife each time to limit the wounds. My hand and fingers were cut severely.

Blood covered my clothes, my face, my hands, and the floor. There was so much blood, I was afraid I was going to bleed to death. I lost a finger and the others were barely still attached, so I tried kicking. Perro stabbed me in the legs and buttocks.

At one point, I wrestled the knife away from him with my good hand. Just as I did, one my neighbors - an older woman - came into view, right before she slammed a chair across Perro's head and shoulders. Warding off that blow, he grabbed her with one arm and flung her across the room, like a laundry bag. She scrambled to her feet and ran out of the apartment.

"Hello! Hello! This is the 911 Operator. If you can hear me, hold on... we're sending assistance right away."

As weak as I was, I was determined not to give in. Or give up. I had come too far to let that son-of-a-bitch Perro take it all away -- not without fighting for my life!

5

The knife was in my good hand, but I didn't have any strength to try to stab him, even though he was lying on top of me.

Perro yanked the electric cord out of the window air-conditioner and began wrapping it around my neck. Then he started to choke me.

He took the knife away from me and, to confirm just how crazed he was at the moment, he stabbed me a few more times. I don't know how many times he stabbed me before I passed out, or what happened after I did. I also don't know if my passing out made him think I was dead.

To be honest, I didn't even remember passing out. The last thing I do remember is feeling very, very tired, so tired that I just had to close my eyes. They were so heavy I just couldn't hold them open any longer. I closed my eyes and drifted into a heavy, dense, wet fog.

For all I know, Perro did think I was dead and then simply walked out of the apartment.

Chapter 2
FIRST INFLUENCES

I was only two when my mother left my father. She was the shiksa in his tight knit Jewish family. Dad's parents never got over his poor choice in a wife and made it perfectly clear to anyone who would listen that Pennsylvania Dutch Betty was unquestionably a reject. I figure that's when the revenge cycle must have begun.

One day, in a fit of hurt and anger, Betty abruptly collected my three-year-old brother Ivan, our nanny Lulu and me from the beautiful waterfront house we loved and moved us into an unfurnished, small, five-room house where we slept for months on a blanket on the floor. She was not concerned about our well being by any stretch of the imagination, but tried to appear so as she began the long process of extracting money for child support and alimony. Betty had determination, fueled by revenge and a bit of a greedy streak.

It was Lulu who mothered me in those days. Before we moved, Ivan and I experienced some artificial idyllic times on the beach with Mom and Dad. Metaphorically, when we would walk up the steps to the house we'd be met by dozens of crabs clicking their pinchers. Lulu-the-Protector would greet us with her broom-weapon and clear a safe path, grabbing a few of them to throw in the pot for dinner. Though Lulu couldn't defend herself from her brutal, wife-beating husband, she did her best to protect me. I would sit on her ample lap while she affectionately buckled my little sandals. She would steal a kiss on my cheek before letting me down. Betty, on the other hand, did not coddle. A good example of Betty's child rearing method is how she taught us to swim. One day, on impulse, she picked us both up and tossed her little two and three-year-old in the pool, deciding that whoever could wriggle out of the deep end, won.

I learned a lot from those two women.

Betty was a beauty. She had a dancer's body, strong brown eyes, short black hair and striking cheekbones that supported her exquisite face. In between bouts of relentless fighting with my father for more money, she financially supported us by donning her hot pants, go-go boots, sparkly top and wig-of-the-night to roam the Poodle Lounge at the Fontainebleau Hotel. She sold cigarettes and took photographs of the happy patrons.

My dad had a cabana at the same prestigious hotel. Sometimes we would stay with him playing with the elevator and cabana boys all day and then get delivered back to Lulu in the early evening just as my mother was heading out the door. Mother finished working around three in the morning, but would continue dancing and dating until six.

Most mornings, Lulu would come in and slip my socks on while I was still in bed and then help me get dressed for kindergarten. At first, she walked me to school. Betty quickly squashed that. With her "sink or swim" approach to life, Mom decided I should get my own tush to school. Ivan was in first grade and went to another school. My kindergarten was at the Methodist Church the other direction, so I walked alone.

The neighborhood was not exactly on the safe side - it was riddled with pedophiles. Often various creepy men in their old cars would follow me along the road. There were no sidewalks, so they would slow down to a snail's crawl and come very close to me. Once in awhile they would ask me to stop and get in the car. I knew better, though. The weird look on their faces as I ran past was startling - even to someone too little to know exactly what they were doing inside of their cars. Even then I understood the disturbing looks on their faces, a look which portrayed an evil intent. It was especially evident when that look was accompanied by rustling, jittery activity in their laps. Sometimes they would get so close; I could see them doing it. Though I wished Lulu would go back to walking me to school, I knew better than to ask my mom.

When we weren't playing at the pool or studying in school, we sat long hours in the courtroom. Using us as pawns in their chess game was the name of my parents' war. Whenever it was a visitation day with Dad, Mom would dress us in the worst clothes she had set aside for that special occasion. I usually wore something of Ivan's that needed to be belted or it would fall off my tiny frame. Neither of us wore shoes for the visitation. It was part of good old greedy Betty's strategy to force my dad into buying us clothes so she didn't have to. Of course, Dad would not be seen with such pitiful waifs and he'd take Ivan shopping. He didn't care for me, to put it mildly. I think it was because I was a spitting image of the woman he detested more than anyone. I was a Baby Betty with my short black hair and big brown eyes; therefore, he was repulsed by me. More times than I'd like to remember, he would have me wait outside the department store while he lavished my brother with clothes and gifts. Ivan favored my father in looks. So in a way, he was treating himself while punishing his ex-wife.

My mom made all my clothes. Whether that's good or bad is highly debatable. They weren't exactly trendy. She told me if I wanted clothes like the other kids or designer jeans, then get a job. I felt like a little clown in the colorful, mismatched patterns made of cheap K-Mart cotton, but at least I didn't have to wear Ivan's hand-me-downs. All new things were kept at my father's place. No way was Dad letting Betty get her hands on anything. We had "Mom clothes" and "Dad clothes" and in between clothes, which were my garish clown clothes.

The hatred and revenge continued. My father kept a private detective on payroll, hoping to catch my mother at something - anything - to get her off his back. He had a successful pickle business, with factories in Russia and Cuba; the biggest one being in Opalocka, Florida. She wanted as much as she could get from his success.

By the time I was six, I was testifying on the witness stand as to the character of my father and mother. I had not bonded with either and didn't know who to pander to so I just followed each lawyer's leading questions. Truth be told, I wanted to please them both - being a little child and needing each one to love and accept me. This was just a fantasy.

I never stopped the fruitless mission of trying to get my father to accept me. I would be as perfect as I could muster whenever I was with him. When he would take us to the factory, and would show Ivan off to everyone, while I was made to wait alone in his office, I was the best "waiting daughter" ever.

To this day, it is impossible to imagine having a mom who would set aside greed and revenge to create a new life for herself and her children. That was never Betty's goal. No one was going to get away without giving her what she declared she deserved. It didn't matter if her kids paid the price.

If the judge had given us the choice of which one I wanted to be reared by, I think I would have picked Lulu.

My first grade put on the play Little Red Riding Hood. Away from both my parents I was outgoing and quite a ham, so my teacher gave me the lead. I just loved it. As I stood behind the curtain, my dark eyes peering out of my little red cloak, I was poised and ready to take my basket to Grandma's house. I had helped my teacher organize all the other players. I had not only memorized my lines very quickly, but knew everyone else's, too. I stepped out onto the stage and had begun skipping through the pretend forest, when to my complete surprise I saw three women sitting together in the first row. There were two milky white beauties on either side of a big beaming black one - my Aunt Eve, Lulu and my mother. I puffed up with pure happiness when they giggled each time I prompted the others with their lines. This was one of those rare moments in my life when the pride of a young girl shone.

My school conducted an annual contest selling candy to raise money to for library books and sports and science equipment. Thanks to my mom's robust ambition and my outgoing personality, I was always the winner. Every year of my elementary life, I won a new bike. It was the same bike each year - same make same color. Once in a while they were a little bigger, but that was the only variation.

Since my mom was always in a competitive mood, she let me go with her to the hotel with cases of the chocolates. Celebrities like Frank Sinatra and his entourage bought several boxes. My brother tagged along and did his best, but he was a bit of an introvert and let me take over in the day-to-day sales department. I should say night-to-night because, after peddling our goods, we were instructed to sleep in the darkroom where Mom developed her photographs of the smiling couples. We'd go back home with her at six or seven in the morning and get ready for school. At 2:00PM, right after we were let out, Mom would take us to the neighborhood check-cashing store frequented by the neighborhood drunks. She pushed us as if we were making a profit or something.

Much later in life, I would be grateful that my mom influenced me in the art of sales. Soon enough I would use those competitive skills to my advantage.

Lulu had Mondays off. Every time she came back to us from spending Sunday nights and Monday with her drunken husband, she would be broken somewhere. Purple swollen eyes, broken arms and bruised parts were displayed every Tuesday morning. Some would heal by Sunday only to be torn up and exposed again the following Tuesday. Lulu was a large woman. She must have weighed closed to three hundred pounds and it was difficult to imagine how a man could actually get around her. For the most part, she would ignore the pain, but when I would outright ask about a particularly nasty sore, she would chastise in her deep southern voice, "Chile, nevah let a man do dis to you." It was heartbreaking.

The only way to ease her pain was to drink. Once my mom went off to work, she would pull out her hidden bottles of Old Milwaukee Beer and begin medicating. She'd be asleep in the chair by eight, so Ivan and I put ourselves to bed whenever we felt like it. As we got older and Lulu's drinking increased, my mom let her go. This was an extremely sad day in my life. No one cuddled and spoiled me like Lulu did. It was the end of knowing someone was looking out for me. It was the end of feeling protected.

Chapter 3
RED MARE

My passion for horses started when I was two or three and my mother put me on a pony. My love for the elegant creatures stayed alive like a pilot light inside me, and by the time I turned ten all burners were on high. I could see the ranches from the freeway and wondered what it would be like to own one of the lovely beasts. As I was headed home from school, I started going out of my way to bicycle by a big ranch in order to get closer to them. One day I just rode down the long driveway toward where ten horses were lined up, each wearing their western saddle. They were tack horses, reluctantly ready to take anyone with twenty-five dollars on a nice little trail ride. Earl was the old man in charge. His long, wispy, white hair blew about in the wind under his beat up, red cowboy hat. He might not have been so scary looking if he had had teeth.

"Excuse me, sir," I said, straddling another new bike. "Can I ride one of your horses?"

"Ya got twenty-five bucks?" he answered and then spat onto the ground near my front tire.

"No," I sighed, then simply turned around and headed home.

The next day I considered passing the ranch by, but couldn't resist trying again. Earl watched me as I rode up to the barn. The horses looked somewhat tired and bedraggled, but in the eyes of a poor ten-year-old, they were majestic.

"Sir, seeing as how nobody is riding any of your horses, couldn't I just ride one – just for a little while?"

"Ya got twenty-five bucks?" He raised one furry, gray eyebrow and spat again.

"No." I tried not to sound pitiful.

On the third day, I was more determined than ever. "Okay. What can I do to earn myself a ride?" I asked using my candy sales voice.

"Have you ever cleaned out a stall, little lady?"

"No, but I could learn."

"Tell you what. If you clean out these here stalls, you can ride Red Mare when you're done," he said with a twinkle.

Red Mare was a skinny chestnut with an easygoing personality. I fell in love with her at first sight. I stroked her muzzle and promised her I would take good care of her after I finished mucking out the stalls.

I began with enthusiasm, knowing that in a little while I would be living my dream of riding a real horse. I worked hard and was careful to do everything Earl told me to do. There were thirty-five of them! The stalls were filled with white sand and I had to pick up piles and piles of poop with the pitchfork and put it into a broken wheelbarrow, leaving as much sand behind as possible so I wouldn't have to put more of it in later. I thought it would be easy because someone had cleaned them in the morning and all I had to do was pick it up again. However, the first person didn't do a very good job and I found myself working even harder to make Earl happy. By the time I finished, the sun was almost down and I had to get home for dinner before mom went to work. Tired and disappointed, I vowed to do better the next day.

I was resolute in getting to the ranch as early as possible, cleaning all the stalls as quickly as I could, and then stepping up and on Red Mare to experience what it would be like to ride my dear horse. As soon as the final school bell buzzed, I peddled like crazy to the farm, gave Red Mare a nice little pet, grabbed the pitchfork and started sifting. Again, before I got to stall number thirty-four, the sun was threatening to set. The look on my face

14

must have said it all because as I got back on my bike, Earl told me that the next day I could ride first and clean the stalls later.

I could hardly sleep that night. It's all I really wanted in life. I pretended Red Mare was my very own horse. And when I finally mounted her later the next day, I felt like a princess sitting atop a champion. I was so starry-eyed; I didn't notice she was limping. I was regal and so was she as we strode around a short trail. Every cell in my body was happy.

I don't know what Earl was thinking because he tried to get me to clean all thirty-five again. I told him about my strict curfew and we finally came to an agreement that I would clean fifteen and ride every day.

Like most of Earl's horses, Red Mare was skinny. After a while, I began to feel bad for riding her. She was working too hard for me. I loved her so much. Every time I came up to the barn, she would bob her head with excitement. We brought each other pure joy. Still limping and emaciated, I had to figure out a way to make her mine.

"Earl, I was wondering if there is a way you would give me Red Mare."

He lifted his bushy eyebrows at my audacity.

"C'mon Earl. She's lame. No one's gonna choose her. She's done plenty of work for you over the years, but it's time to take her off the line. I would take good care of her, you know that. Please?" I was putting every bit of pleading and sadness in my scrunched up face.

"What would you do with her?" That was closer to a "no" statement than a question, but I would not give up.

"I'll go back to cleaning all thirty-five stalls and pay you to put her in your pasture if you'll let me. Please, PLEASE?" I was desperate. I needed to protect her.

Earl squinted back, "If you clean all them stalls you won't have time to ride anymore."

"I know." I was willing to give up the joy of riding in order to make Red Mare feel better.

"Well, okay, but how're you gonna feed her?"

Now, that was a good question, but I didn't let him think I wasn't prepared for it. He finally agreed when I told him I was getting a babysitting job. Then I simply went about the business of getting myself that job.

There were these four girls whose family was rich enough for each of them to take riding lessons at very young ages. I approached their mother and was hired immediately to come four nights a week.

By the time I was eleven, my days consisted of getting up and going to school, riding my candy-drive bike to the ranch, mucking out thirty-five dirty stalls, spoiling Red Mare with carrots and kisses, going home and having dinner with Mom and Ivan, promising Mom to be in bed by eight - and then playing football till long after eight with the neighborhood boys. They all had to wait for me because I was their quarterback.

Earl's pasture board was the cheapest way to go, so I put *my* horse out all day and brought her in to feed again at night. I did this every day so she didn't lose any weight. She was so happy to be retired and grazing among the other retired horses. And I was happy to work so Red Mare would feel loved.

This was a period when my brother really annoyed me. Mom tried several new babysitters after Lulu, but none were a fit. So, by the time I was eleven and Ivan was twelve, we were on our own.

When we were younger I was his subordinate, especially according to my parents. But when we were alone, he was simply benign. He was quiet and kept to himself. By the time he was twelve, though still a loner, he got restless and I became his target.

From the minute he got home from school until he fell asleep, Ivan watched wrestling on the television. In the comfort of our small house, this is when Ivan the Introvert became Ivan the Terrible. He didn't have any friends, he wasn't interested in anything else and so he waited every night for me to come in from playing football with the neighborhood boys to practice his moves on me. He beat the shit out of me every night. I would tell my mother, but it was a waste of time since Ivan could do no wrong in Mom's eyes.

After a long day of school, babysitting and mucking out stalls, I would come home, lock myself in my room and climb out my bedroom window to go play football or hang out in the streets. I would then climb back in around midnight to avoid Ivan.

Ivan wasn't the only misfit in school. Though I had the ambition to make friends, at eleven, I was small and boyish with crooked teeth. I used to come home depressed and sometimes crying. My mother told me it's not how big you are, it's how smart you are. So off I'd go to fight the world one more day.

My real friends were the horses. I lived for them. I found several ways to work for Earl including riding the other kids' muscular and stately horses when they didn't show up for lessons. Those horses needed a regular workout every day and I jumped at the chance to be the one to make sure they got thoroughly exercised. I got paid handsomely for it as well.

Sometimes I would use the money to buy a nice pair of jeans so I could fit in more at school, but I would have to wait till I grew out of the gawky stage and into my looks before the friends would come. Meanwhile, the horses did the job.

Chapter 4
AMAZON

The ranch had several characters roaming its grounds. That's where I met Paul Purdy. Purdy he was a skinny, old, hunched, dried apple faced exercise rider-turned-pony boy - although the title "boy" was a misnomer. He had several stalls, a paddock and quite a few horses. One day he brought out this gorgeous, feisty gelding named Amazon. This animal, a golden Palomino with a shimmering white mane and tail was breathtaking. Purdy was having a horrendous time taming Amazon. He would rear and lunge and give his owner all kinds of fits. That's where I learned most of my cuss words. After several weeks of this bad behavior, Purdy was losing patience and asked me if I would try to break him. Now either Purdy had it out for me, or thought I was one hell of a good rider. Who asks an inexperienced eleven-year-old stall mucker to take on such a huge and dangerous job? I didn't give him time to think about it and hopped up on Amazon as fast as I could. He reared and bucked and then let me ride him. I rode this spirited gelding every day until he and I spoke the same language. It didn't happen right away, though. Mr. Amazon had a mind of his own. One day I had had it with his rearing ways and I cracked an egg right on top of his unruly head. That sure surprised him. He never reared after that.

He and I became great friends. As I grew closer to Amazon, Purdy grew distant. He said he no longer had use for him. I was amazed. I rode him home one day, much to my mother's consternation. Our small house sat on a good size property with a yard full of grass that Amazon would love to munch on I had not bothered to tell her I owned a couple of horses. But once I explained how I was paying for them with my own money, she was fine.

I even got to ride him in the Fourth of July parade. He was so handsome in his blue fur tack and saddle pad. This horse had a lot of spunk left, which I proved by entering him in several barrel races. He became a champion. And I became an excellent rider.

I had done a variety of jobs at the ranch by the time I was thirteen. My favorite one was to ride the horses that belonged to lazy rich kids. They were a few years older than me and all they wanted to do was smoke pot. Paul Purdy was their supplier. The girls - Judy, Deb, Diane and Katy would smoke and flirt with Billy, Sam and George behind the barn while I got atop of some of the noblest thoroughbreds I could ever hope to ride. I couldn't imagine why the kids would waste their money to pay someone to ride them when they could be enjoying the beauties themselves. It was a perfect situation for me, though. The more often I would take one out, the better my skills became. The spoiled rich girls and boys, Purdy, their trainer/dealer, and their amazing horses, and I were all very satisfied. And it got even better.

One day while I was in the tack room, I found half of a joint on the floor in the corner. Curious, I opened it up. To uneducated me, it just looked like hay. Later that same day, I convinced my mom to drive me over to the Country Western Feed House to buy a bale of real good alfalfa hay because I want to spoil Red Mare and Amazon. As I was putting the bale in the tack room, a few loose leaves fell on the floor. I thought - wait a minute... that hay looks just like the pot. Then I conjured up this idea to play a joke on the rich kids. I mean what the hell - they were so full of themselves with their weed and their exclusive group in their trendy designer jeans and fancy riding clothes, I figured it would be fun to pull

19

one over on the ones who looked at me like I was just the dumb rider. Even if I had been a little older, I would never have fit in with them. I looked like a boy with crooked teeth and though I had those gorgeous, large, brown eyes I inherited from my mother, it was all out of proportion and not even close to pretty. I was a stable boy, and as long as I had my horses and my ambition, I could take it. So, what would be the harm in a little joke?

The alfalfa was too moist, so I put a generous handful on a plate and dried it in a secret spot in the sun.

The going rate for Purdy's pot was five dollars a joint. My sizeable handful in a baggie could provide twenty or thirty. I started the ruse by telling Deb that I had my own resources and that she could buy a whole baggie of some special Hawaiian weed for twenty-five dollars. She shrugged her shoulders as if to say, "Why not?" Then gave me thirty and told me to keep the change. I giggled to myself at the thought of those guys going behind the barn, sucking in hay and coughing all over themselves.

I was surprised when Deb came back a couple hours later just to tell me how good it was and how everybody got really stoned. I thought she was pulling one on me. I laughed as though I was saying, "Okay, we're even." But she meant it. She seriously loved the alfalfa and said some of the others wanted to buy their own baggies of the Hawaiian. What? Either they had been smoking hay all along or my horses were eating marijuana. This was crazy. I waited several days because I wasn't sure if they weren't all in on an elaborate joke on me. But Will and George took me aside and said they seriously would pay me a little more if I would score for them. So, I asked my mom if she would kindly take me to the feed store again. That was the beginning of me becoming the biggest alfalfa cartel in town. I figured I was doing them a favor in the end - after all, I was saving them from a drug addiction.

For quite a long time, I was the main supplier to just about every junior high and high school stoner on my side of town. My horses were happily dining on the good alfalfa hay while I separated the imposter pot to dry out and be sold.

I kept a few joints in my tack box in case someone new wanted to try the Hawaiian. One day one of the little girls I babysat was looking for a band aide when she found a joint. I didn't realize she had snuck it in her pocket until her mother came pounding on the front door of my house demanding to see my mother. She was ranting about what a horrible influence I was on her children. She said she had taken the alfalfa joint to the police to have it analyzed and that it turned out to be a marijuana cigarette. She fired me on the spot and slammed the door as she exited our living room.

My mother glared at me. I could see her blood pressure rising. "How dare you! That's it! No more horses. You are never going to that ranch again. EVER! I'm taking away your bike, your privileges, and your free time. How could you do this to me?"

"But Mom..."

"You will go directly to school and come home directly afterward. I will have months of work for you to do here, young lady." She was just beginning.

"But Mom, that's not marijuana," I said most sincerely.

"Do you think I'm some kind of idiot, Gigi?"

"No, but it's *not pot*." Pause. "It's hay." Pause. For a minute I thought she was going to take a swing at me. "Mom, remember the hay I've been buying?" I didn't give her time to answer, "Well, I bought it for Amazon in the first place, but then I thought it looked like the pot the rich kids were always smoking, so I tried to play a joke on them. Only they really, really liked it. So I just put it in baggies and kept selling it to them, and Amazon gets the rest. It's not marijuana. It's alfalfa. Everybody's happy." Pause. "Well, until now. Linda's mother is not happy... but she's wrong"

She was dumbfounded. She just stood there trying to make sense of it. So, I grabbed her hand, dragged her to my room, and pulled open a large dresser drawer to expose an immense amount of ten and twenty dollar bills - filled to the brim. Now she was dumbfounded.

"Mom, I have so much money I don't even know what to do with it. Why don't I buy you a nice, new microwave oven?" Pause. "And a dishwasher?"

I was right back in business.

Chapter 5
RACE HORSES

Nothing got in the way of my devotion to the horses and strengthening my riding skills. I studied everything I could and took practice seriously. At fourteen, I was quite an athlete. I barrel raced and broke two-year-olds to prepare them for the track. I even raced for money down the backstretch at the ranch against other teenagers who were probably stoned. This stirred a new desire in me. I wanted to be a jockey. It became an obsession. School was very low on my priority list, but if I could be a jockey I would be so proud to be in one of the coolest professions, combining my competitive nature and my small, childlike frame with my passion for horses. It was the answer to everything. I would do whatever it took to make this happen.

My best friends at that time were Diane and her sister Terri. Their father was a trainer on the track and their brother was a jockey. It was perfect - two best friends with a very cute jockey brother. I had a huge crush on him. He didn't pay much attention to me, although I'm sure he could see my blatant affection for him. I had a feeling he might have sex with me, but I was still a virgin and was embarrassed that I didn't know very much about it. So, with the nerve only a naïve teen could conjure up, I asked a very popular boy named Johnny to explain it all to me. I played football with him almost every night and always thought he was so handsome. He had a lot of sexual experience, as he was popular all over the neighborhood - and the whole town, for that matter. We were football buddies and I trusted him to give me the straight answers. So, after a game he told me to go home and he would come over and explain it to me. I was so excited and ready for the kind of talk I should have had with parents. He arrived and I was taken aback seeing him standing there looking so fine.

Ivan was in bed. Good.

Johnny walked in and curtly said, "What time will your parents be home?"

As I began to answer, "My mom works nights and..." he moved close to me, took off his pants and mine. I had only a few seconds to appreciate how handsome and popular he was before he was on top of me, and then instant penetration. Flash. Just like that. It hurt! But I didn't scream - I didn't want Ivan to come in - and besides, Johnny had his hand over my mouth. Before I knew it, he was up, pulling his pants on and saying, "Well, see ya around, kid."

I hardly knew what happened, but was quite happy not to be a virgin anymore. I figured that was the main reason no one paid much attention to me. I was going on fifteen and finally had sex. Now I was free to flirt.

Dying for attention, I began with Diane and Terri's brother. My newfound deflowering gave me confidence. I could tell it was working because he finally noticed me.

One night he came over and we talked for a minute or two about racing. Then he kissed me. I thought that was good. He then quickly yanked my pants down, unzipped his pants, pulled out his penis and stuck it between my legs. My jeans were so tight I could hardly move, as he didn't pull them down very far. This version was strange. It was not like the other experience. I didn't feel anything. He seemed to be struggling to get himself organized. I didn't know till later that he had never had sex before and had no clue what to do. As far as I was concerned, the jury was out regarding the pleasure part of "making love".

After that he brought over another jockey friend named Samuel. We did the same thing. I didn't know what was going on, but I was happy that boys were paying attention to me.

I was running the two-year-olds when I met Jim, another son of a racehorse owner. He always watched while I was working and soon we became friends. My boyish figure was starting to change. I had nice sized breasts, thin legs and my bottom had developed nicely from all the riding. Around twenty, he was way too old for me. He was a bit of a dork and a loser, did a lot of drugs and had no ambition whatsoever. My sights were clearly set on becoming a jockey. Still, he had a big old crush on me.

And a car.

Jim was fun. He drove me wherever I needed to go and even gave me high-grade feed he stole from his dad's racehorses.

There was only one way an "almost fifteen-year-old" could get a job at the racetrack and that was to stand out front of the track entrance, much like the day workers do in front of Home Depot, and wait and hope someone would hire a few of us for the day. The hardest part was that you had to be there by 4:00 in the morning. I begged my mom to come straight home from work and take me to the track so I could finish before school started.

On the first day my bubble was popped when no one picked me. I then had to call my mom to turn around and pick me back up. On the second day, I had a little more hope. I figured people would recognize me from the day before and be inclined to choose me. Mom dutifully came home from the Poodle Lounge in time to get me there by 3:45. I eagerly waited and was once again overlooked. Undaunted, I kept it up until on the fifth day a man named Dave Harper called me over. I told him I'd do anything to work my way toward being a jockey. He said I could start by mucking stalls. Of course, what else? But now I was at the track. I knew if I had the chance to get on a horse one day and show my talent, someone would notice me, and my world would change forever.

Dave Harper had two sons around my age who didn't seem normal. They mostly slept in the back of his truck under the camper shell. On the occasions they appeared for breakfast or lunch, they were both exceptionally shy and introverted - even timid, like beaten animals.

Dave also had an exercise boy with him, who was every bit as weird as the sons, but at least he was cute. I wished he would look at me, but he was very shy and only had riding on his mind. So it turned out that since we were so alike, we were competitors. But there was something else about this boy. It often seemed like he was trying to warn me about something. It was like he would almost get the courage to tell me and then think better of it. I figured it had to be about those weird sons of Dave's that were curled up under the camper shell all day.

After a few months of regular work at the track, I was on my way to fulfilling my dream to become a jockey. Dave was making me do everything from the ground up, but I didn't care. I worked hard and was fast and reliable. I must have asked him every single day if I could ride one of the horses. I knew I had the experience and talent and wanted a chance to show them off. The problem was I was too young to be working there. I lied of course, but the truth was I was not quite fifteen and you had to be at least sixteen.

Soon I was walking the hots. That's when a horse has finished working out and needs someone to walk them around the shed row for a couple of hours to cool them down. I finished by 7:30 - just in time for Jim to give me a ride to high school.

School was the worst part of my day. I was ostracized for being the poor kid that needed to have a job. Still wearing handmade clothes from cheap fabric, I stood out among the hip leather aviator jackets and acid washed jeans. My grades were not good. I didn't understand why they were teaching all this stupid stuff like literature, chemistry and history while they did not offer me one class on how to make a living and manage my money. So I went to the counselor to see if I could go on a work release program. I wanted to get credits for working. She found a way to manipulate the system. I was grateful and especially relieved because I got a pass to get out early to resume work.

Dave Harper was an older man with sloppy blond hair, a large belly and an evil eye. From the first day I met him at the racetrack, he would "accidentally" touch me inappropriately. I hated it, but I wasn't supposed to be working in the first place. Who would I complain to? One day I was in the tack room and Dave came in right behind me. He quickly closed the door behind him, dropped his pants and demanded that I give him a blowjob. I was horrified and stood there frozen. Then someone knocked loudly on the door and he pulled his pants right up. I urgently escaped the tack room and felt everyone's eyes on me. I think everyone knew he was some sort of pedophile. I was grateful for the person who knocked. Someone was protecting me.

After that, I kept my distance as much as I could. Sometimes he would come out of nowhere and brush up real close. It was like he was continuously waiting for a moment to ambush and touch me. Using my fifteen-year-old logic and manipulative skills, I finally led him on to think that if he let me ride a horse, we would then talk about sexual favors. I was convinced that someone would swoop me away from Lecherous Dave Harper the moment they saw my talent.

The day came. I had begged Dave in front of some other people and he reluctantly agreed. He gave me one of the three-year-olds that had been laid up from an injury for a while. I didn't care - it was my first break. As I mounted this beauty, exhilaration took over. Finally, it was my chance to shine. I started him at a nice jog - the two of us feeling real good. I loved that sensation - the adrenalin and satisfaction that merges when the rhythm of horse and rider are in sync.

Then, my horse tripped on something and went down on his knees and on his side. As he came up, he smashed me in the face with his head. That instant I broke my nose, but a bigger problem was in play - my foot was caught in the stirrup as he righted himself and began to run around the racetrack dragging me on the ground. As he gained speed, he stayed close to the rail, so my body was not only being torn up by the track itself, but the wooden rail was piercing my sides and back.

I woke up in the hospital paralyzed. My body was raw from the rail, disks in my spine were twisted and hemorrhaging, and there were pins in my feet. I was told I would not walk again, but on the third day, inexplicably, all the feeling came back. I had no money or insurance, so my mom and I looked to Dave for workman's comp, only to find he didn't have any. He knew he was in trouble and skipped town. My mother sued him and we won a judgment of twenty thousand dollars. We never found him, though, and we never saw a penny of it. So that left me with a pile of medical bills. I wanted to get him where it hurt - in his wallet - because I wanted to stop him from ever hurting any little boys or girls again. We never saw him again and mom looked to me to pay my own bills. So, back to work it was.

Chapter 6
ALMOST INDEPENDENT

I was not doing well in the eighth grade. While trying to heal from the traumatic accident on the racetrack, I was lonely, missed my horses, had no friends and could not concentrate on schoolwork.

My brother never fit in, either. After middle school, my mother got the court to make my father pay for a private school for him in nearby Hollywood. It was filled with kids who were different and shy - and maybe a little weird. It didn't take too long before Ivan made several friends. This seemed like a much better situation for me, too. I pleaded with my mother to let me go to Ivan's school, but my father would not pay for me. It had been like this all my life. He simply hated me and adored Ivan. It was a fact of life I had to accept, but I never, ever knew why.

I begged and begged my mom to let me go to Ivan's school. Finally, I struck up a deal to make it happen. The local K-Mart was just down the street from the private school. I promised to get a job, pay off my medical bills and pay half my tuition. Mom went along with it. They hired me right away. Once again, I had to lie about my age, as I was only fifteen and a half.

Ivan had a friend named Albert who had a huge crush on me. His family owned a carnival that set up at a nearby church once a year. He had greasy blonde hair, really bad teeth, and spoke like his mouth was always full. Needless to say, I did not share his feelings, but I did take advantage of him. I was not yet old enough to drive and needed him to take me everywhere. He was sort of a fool in that respect. I would call him in the middle of the night to go to the store and bring me some cookies while I played with neighborhood boys. He would accommodate me with cheerfulness. Since I promised my mom I would keep up my grades in this new school, I also had Albert do all my homework.

I was a cashier at K-Mart. My academic schedule was extremely lenient so it was easy to get a lot of hours in at work. I had my learners permit to drive, so mom would let me practice driving with her to school and Albert would take me home. I promised myself I would save money to buy my own car so I didn't have to depend on anyone anymore.

I worked extremely hard. Maybe it was from the influence of the candy sales experience or perhaps I had inherited some of my mom's determination, but when I set my sights on a goal, I could not be distracted. I noticed most of the other workers were on the lazy side. They would take quite a lot of breaks and dawdle around. They complained a lot, too. I did not relate to their attitude at all. I was there to make money in order to pay bills, go to the kind of school I preferred and to get myself a dependable car. K-Mart was as good as any vessel to get me moving closer to my goal. No complaints from me.

The store got extremely busy during the holiday season and the winter flu seemed to be hitting everyone in town. One day the stock clerk just didn't show up, and then the head cashier didn't make it. Before I knew it, I was running the whole store. I had the same flu as everyone else in town - working with a temperature of 102 degrees - but I didn't give up. I had a job to do and an obligation to keep. I pushed through the fevers and headaches and worked many days overtime because it was just the right thing to do. After the holidays my bosses made me head cashier. Most people can work there for ten years before they get a promotion like that.

After a few months I met a boy named Matt and we fell in love. Matt was tall and thin with long black hair and big brown eyes. After dating so many jockeys, Matt seemed much taller than he really was. He was the manager of the stock department. He wasn't the cutest boy I had ever seen, but he was cute enough and he was nice to me. He lived just down the street from K-Mart. We were inseparable. I wasn't sure about his future - an eighteen-year-old working at K-mart and living with his mother didn't hold much promise, but it was okay for the moment.

Matt and I had a lot of sex. Being with him was a whole new way of making love. Even though we were not all that experienced, it was warm and fun, intimate and delightful. He was madly in love with me. We would lie next to each other and he would talk about our future and marriage and kids - it was that euphoria of a first love.

About five months into our relationship, I got pregnant. This was absolutely not acceptable to me. I was going to turn sixteen in a few weeks and had a lot to do to ensure I had a good future. He wanted to get married and have the kid. This was not my plan *at all*. I almost had enough money to buy my first car; I was ready for my independence and I wanted an abortion. Matt would not hear of it. We had a big argument. I made it very clear that I was going to have an abortion - with or without him.

Fate intervened and - I ran into an old girlfriend from the track and she told me where to have it done.

On my sixteenth birthday, I got my driver's license, bought my first car and drove myself to the clinic to get an abortion. I had no regrets. I was back in control of my own future.

Matt called to talk some sense into me. I told him it was done. He was enraged. He said he would get even with me. I kept my distance from him after that. He was so angry and I didn't want to put myself where he could get agitated. I changed my hours at work and did whatever I could to avoid him.

I was born a driven soul. Perhaps the fact that my prosperous father denied everything to me, or my mother insisted that I earn my own way, or that I always felt alone in my journey - but no person, no eighteen-year-old stock boy, and certainly no unwanted pregnancy, was going to slow me down from being independent and wealthy.

One day I was thinking about how weird things were between my father and me. Sure, I looked like Mom, but I was still his offspring and I couldn't comprehend what would make him feel such hatred towards me and such love towards Ivan. My mom assured me that I was definitely his child, so why would he so transparently favor one over the other? He never got to know me. He never wanted to. The whole relationship was bothering me. I didn't want him to remember his only daughter as the reject he and Betty spawned. I had grown and changed and I wanted to make a new impression. No, I *needed* to make a new impression.

On my next day off, I went down to Bal Harbor to the restaurant he partially owned, walked in the door and there he was. It was quite a moment - still frozen in my mind - the two of us silently staring at one another like stray cats that couldn't decide if the other was a potential enemy. He had not seen me since I was a squirrelly-looking, scrawny eleven-year-old. I stood there, heart about to bounce out of my rib cage, trying to look confident in my expensive designer jeans and classy silk top, presenting a small smile on the face of what was now a young woman. He looked handsome to me. As I moved toward him, he took my cue and moved toward me. And then we hugged. I think it was the first time that ever happened. That moment changed my life.

We talked for hours. I told him all the things I had done and worked toward. I told him I bought my own car and had a job and was helping put myself through school. For the very first time in my life, he said he was proud of me. He admired me for being so responsible. With all the enthusiasm a young teen uses to impress someone important, I told him I wanted to be rich like him and drive a Cadillac and have a cabana... and horses. He smiled and gave me a little loving wink. My heart did a flip.

He introduced me to all his friends as a proud father would. It was amazing. He was nothing like the man I knew from my childhood. I spent the whole day with him. It was intoxicating to finally be recognized as a real, contributing, responsible *daughter*. I could tell he was thrilled, too. We made plans to have lunch again the next day.

I went to sleep dreaming of all the things I could do to prove to my father that I was worthy of this new pride. My whole life was ahead of me and now that I finally had a connection to such an important person. I was ready to take on the world.

At 3:00 AM the following morning my mother woke me by anxiously shaking my shoulder and told me to come with her into Ivan's room. She told my brother and me that Dad had had a heart attack and died on the way to the hospital. I thought it was a bad dream.

We were not a talkative family and the one person we never talked about was my father. But with this shocking news, the three of us sat on Ivan's bed and talked until the sun came up.

My heart and spirit were devastated. The potential for a relationship had been enormous and now it was never going to be more than what had occurred the day before. I was grateful for our one and only connection. At least I had some closure, but my heart ached for all the things I would never be able to impress him with.

Later that morning I was going to pick up my schoolwork then go to work for a few hours, but when I put the key in the ignition the car wouldn't start. After a number of people stopped by to check it out, they determined there was sugar in my gas tank. Matt had told me he would get even.

No father, no boyfriend, no baby, no car.

My mother took me to work.

Chapter 7
MONEY

Still stunned with the news about my father, I pushed through and went to work where I ran into my friend Doris from the racetrack days. She said she was going to move away and wanted to know if I would be interested in her job. She was a secretary for a construction company. I assumed that she must have made a lot of money there because she had nice jewelry, a good car and a decent apartment. The job was in the town of Hialeah, which was a little too far to ride the candy sales bike I had outgrown.

I had started saving some money for another car, so when I told my mom about the new job possibility she took me to the local dealer down the street where I fell in love with a beautiful Cutlass Supreme. I had just enough for the down payment. I got the financing approved, but my mother had to co-sign because I was under eighteen.

I drove away in my brand new car to meet up with Doris, who would introduce me to her boss and see if he would hire me. I needed this job. My small K-Mart salary was not going to pay my debts.

Her boss' name was Charlie. He had a small amount of white hair, a bulging, round belly, milky blue eyes that betrayed his cataracts and smoked like a chimney. Like Charley himself, his clothes were old and his pants had to be held up with suspenders to accommodate the protruding midsection. He was not my idea of what a business mogul would look like but when he opened his mouth he impressed.

Over lunch, I listened as he talked to Doris about some of the buildings they we constructing, those that needed repairs and which building codes needed to be looked into. The more he talked, the more enthusiastic I became. I saw this as the potential for me to sink my teeth into something fresh and stimulating. The bigger the challenge, the more I was attracted to it. Charlie must have noticed my keen interest because he hired me right there on the spot. He offered $400 per week and a gas credit card. He even told me I could start immediately - as in "right then". But I had to let K-Mart know of my intent. I wanted to be ethical in that way.

On the next Monday morning I was surprised to walk into a miniature office barely big enough for the two of us. Where were all the workers and construction bosses? I found out later that they were at the job sites and only came in when we had meetings.

Charlie began showing me the ropes and he was as impressed with my quick mind as I was with his. I was sure this was a perfect move for me. School would simply have to wait.

About four weeks after my father had passed away, we received a letter from his lawyer requesting us to come to his office. My mother was wound up. She had been reminding us our whole lives how rich he was. Now everything was going to change for us. My dad was worth millions. We were his only offspring.

Our meeting was set for three days later. I don't think I slept a wink before the day arrived to go to the lawyer's office. My imagination went wild with what I intended to do with my inheritance. I didn't expect to get millions, but even if it was a hundred thousand or even just ten thousand - I was going to make my portion of the money work to make more money. I understood, more than any sixteen-year-old, about investing in property and creating passive income. I was going to be as rich as my father one day and everyone would be in awe at my financial prowess.

I was a little surprised at how many people were there to hear the reading of the will. The room was so crowded that Mom, Ivan and I had to stand in the very back. I held my breath as the conservator began reading my father's wishes. The majority of the money went to his sister. Next, the lawyer got a handsome amount, then the girlfriend was gifted abundantly, then the secretary and then the brother.

The room was eerily silent as he came to the legal heirs - the children. With a smirk on his face, the attorney read, "I leave to my son Ivan and my daughter Gigi the sum of $1.00 each."

Stunned and humiliated, we left quietly and went back to our little house without speaking a word to one another. My mother crawled into a hole at that point. I don't know what she expected, but I'm sure that was not it. I was appalled that a man could hate his ex-wife so much that he could derive some kind of pleasure in hurting his children. Who was this person? Why had he been so hateful? The one charmed day I had had with my estranged father was not enough to answer my most crucial questions.

My mother's longtime lawyer told her that a man can leave his money to whomever he wants and there was nothing she could do about it. Well, I was not the kind of person who took "there's nothing you can do about it" sitting down. Those kinds of challenges only inspired me. I was not about to let my mother and brother down.

I confided in Charlie and he got a lawyer for us. After a little research, I was informed there was going to be a hearing for the sale of the pickle factory. Apparently, the sister didn't want it and was going to sell everything my dad had worked so hard for. My brother was the only one left to carry the family name, so I made it my priority to figure out how to buy that company.

The notice said the approval for the sale was to happen at 2:00 PM on Monday, so on the Friday prior I struck a deal with Charlie to borrow $25,000, using the factory I was trying to buy as collateral. I was prepared for the hearing. I hoped the judge would be impressed with my good intentions and prayed he would at least hear me out. I had no idea where I was going to find the rest of the money but I didn't care. I was a fearless teenager - and I was not about to crawl into the same hole my mother currently resided in.

Monday finally came. I walked into the courtroom with all the anticipation and courage I could muster up. I addressed the judge and showed him my money and told him about my intentions to keep the business in the family name. I assured him that my brother and I could run the factory - after all, we practically grew up there. I was promising him the world if he would just let me buy the factory. The judge looked at me with a sympathetic smile and said, "Sorry little lady, but that property was sold at 1:00 PM. You are too late."

I was astounded. "I don't understand. The notice said 2:00 PM. Look, I have money and everything!"

"Sorry," he said without emotion.

"But I've been working since I was eleven and I can prove it. I know how to run businesses. K-Mart promoted me when most workers have to wait several years to get promoted," I was talking as fast as I could.

"My brother grew up learning my father's business. He was the heir apparent. You can't take it away from him!" I repeated that I brought some money with me. I needed him to know how organized and serious I was.

The judge did not take pity on me but I continued to argue in sincere sadness.

"Look, Miss Kapchuk, no one here had been informed of your interest in this property. We were ahead of schedule and figured it was fine to just move ahead. I'm sorry you missed it, but you are under age in the first place and we need to move on now."

He then gave me a stern stare and dismissed me. It was at that moment I realized my trip to the courthouse would have been fruitless even if I had made it an hour earlier.

I was beyond angry. I was never really arguing for my brother's sake. He didn't have the drive to make the business grow. But I figured I'd be the one to dig in and kick some ass. That opportunity no longer existed. No matter - I was going to prove to everyone that I would be rich like the man who left me one dollar and that I would drive a Cadillac like I had promised on the only day that now mattered to me.

I was advised to protest the will so it would be tied up in court - a place very familiar to me - for a while. After a month, the sister decided to make us an offer of $10,000 each. We settled.

My brother and I also legally received his social security benefits. That was about $700 per month for each of us. My mother was happy about that, as she kept it for the rent money she had been charging us to live there. The only caveat was that we could only receive that money as long as we stayed in school. It helped her pay for Ivan's private school, but I was no help at all. By the beginning of the 10th grade, I was working full time for Charlie. Sorry, Mom.

Chapter 8
UNDER CONSTRUCTION

As I got into the heart of working for Charlie, he involved me in several principal aspects of his business. I was treated like a smart, capable woman - not a high school dropout who was just about to turn seventeen. With that kind of responsibility, however, came the sexual advances. Charlie's flirting went unnoticed at first because of my drive to learn the business. Looking back, I can see it, but at the time I was a shark devouring as much information as I could and nothing else mattered. And then the gifts started coming. Every time we would win a bid, pass an important inspection, or break ground for more work, he would give me hefty bonuses and buy me nice clothes and even diamonds. Innocently, I believed he celebrated as generously with his wife.

While my days were filled with creating construction work, something new was developing between my mother and me. Once she got over the shunned inheritance debacle and was impressed with the salary and benefits I had coming in, we started hanging out at nightclubs together. She was a dancer so I would follow her footsteps like a best friend. This new version of a mother-daughter relationship was a little odd at first, but I felt more her equal now that I was helping run a legitimate business... and paying rent. We would go from club to club to compete in dance contests. Of course she always beat me, but I kept trying. My competitive side, as well as my need for approval, gave me the motivation. We would dance till dawn then we would go out to breakfast. I'd take her home and then go straight to work. I'd work till five o'clock that night, then go home and nap till around eleven and go out again - always with mom in tow. I acted as if I was twenty-something and belonged in the fast lane. I had a fake I.D. and all the bouncers knew me. When we would enter a nightclub, men thought the Kapchuk sisters were here to party. My mother didn't drink at all, as she was a serious dancer. I, on the other hand, danced for fun. Forget about trying to dance to perfection like Mom. She took it very seriously while I preferred sipping on alcohol and flirting with the DJ. This was a time in my life when I was full of confidence. Men were always trying to date me but I just wanted to be playful. I had no time for serious dating.

One day, Charlie and I were alone in the office and he attempted to put his hands up my skirt and play with himself. I was mortified. I didn't want to lose my job, so I nicely pushed him away and flirted back, letting him think I was a little interested but not ready yet. He took my cue and went back to business.

By the time I was seventeen and a half, I was running the whole office, including the bids and the subcontractors. In between doing the actual work for Charlie, I was also studying business law, real estate, and even studied for my securities license. I was a jack of all studies and master of none. I didn't study anything for long - I just wanted guidelines. I could not afford to take time off work for the full education.

It didn't take long before Charlie made me vice president. Vice president of a successful construction company before I turned eighteen! I considered that to be the stepping stone to creating my own construction company. The only thing stopping me was the license to do so. Clubbing with Mom was put on hold while I continued going to school at night to study building construction and civil engineering. The only girl in those classes, I lied and said I was eighteen and had gotten my GED. I studied day and night and Charlie helped me.

They offered only two tests a year to get your license and the next one was just before I turned eighteen. I figured what the hell and registered for that one. My lies wouldn't matter in a couple of months anyway. I was nervous that the test would be especially hard for me with only a ninth grade education and had no idea how I was going to pull it off, but once the questions came up I felt fine. You didn't have to be Einstein to pass you just needed common sense - and I was full of that. I finished and went back to Charlie to tell him I was sure I got a high mark.

I had been told they would contact me by mail within thirty days. One week later I received a letter. I was so nervous to open it because it came so early. As soon as I saw the words WE ARE SORRY TO INFORM YOU... my heart sank. It went on to say that there was a discrepancy about my age. They admonished me that by law I had to be eighteen to take that test and I would not be allowed to apply again for five years. They closed the letter by saying that lying about my age was a federal offense. Damn.

At least I was still vice president of Charlie's company. The day I turned eighteen, I formed my first corporation using Charlie's license. Because Charlie had a contract with the county he was not allowed to do work for private companies, so I was able to do all the jobs that conflicted.

I went back to working all day and then clubbing all night with Mom. I had enough energy for ten. I was on fire! I still wanted that Cadillac, so Charlie and I went to pick one out. It was a beautiful two-toned, custom-painted Eldorado coupe. Between my dream car, my three hundred dollar outfits, and my killer body, I was unstoppable. Who needed a construction license?

Charlie's obsession for me took a turn for the worse. He started following me to the clubs to see who I was dancing with. He would sit at the back of the bars and watch me with those creepy, milky eyes. He would look for incidences where someone might touch me, and then the next day he would torture me about it. He considered me to be his girlfriend and thought I was just waiting for the right moment for us to be a couple; it didn't matter that he was married. I did not want to put him off because he was my ticket to earning money and learning the business. I readily - and I suppose, selfishly - accepted any and all the expensive gifts he often bought me, telling myself that I "earned" them. My strategy was to keep things light and at bay by slightly flirting and teasing him, suggesting that maybe someday soon I would be ready to be "his". I had a long way to go before I could make good on my promise to myself to be a millionaire like my father and I needed this education, so if I had to move his swollen hands from inappropriate places or walk in a arc around him while batting my long eyelashes, I was willing to do it.

But that's as far as I would ever go.

Chapter 9
RICH MEN

One of our big contracts was the renovation of the Hialeah racetrack. I was excited about this, especially since I got to spend most of my days there checking on the crew... and gambling. I met a small Italian man with longish white hair named Jeff. He was a little scary and intimidating at first, but we had a good rapport. He had this air about him. If I closed my eyes when he was speaking, I swear I could hear the Godfather talking. We would joke about Charlie and the construction crew - making up gangster names for everyone and making fun of them. I didn't quite understand what his job at the track was, but it was clear that he was the kind of guy that got things done. If I told him I was having trouble getting paid from a job, I was paid the next day. If I mentioned I was bidding on a job but I was a little high on my bid, I got the job. I would be so grateful for his help I would give him a "commission", which translated to kicking him back money. It didn't take long before I figured out he was connected, but you don't ask questions when business was booming.

Besides taking care of all my work in construction, I was all over the racetrack. It wasn't long before Jeff had me running numbers - that's when you take bets from people that are not at the track and go to the window for them. I made a nice bit of money, it was convenient and Jeff appreciated it.

Soon we started loaning people money at a very large interest rate with many points. I would put up the money from the 10k I inherited and the money earned in the construction business and Jeff would loan it out and do the collections.

I was carrying around large sums of money at any time, so Jeff got me a 25 automatic revolver which I carried it with me in my purse and car.

This was all exciting and risky - but I didn't realize exactly how dangerous it was. One day I went to pick up the numbers for Jeff to bet at the track, when Charlie had me do something else so I was late to make the bets. The people I was running for had some control of the outcome of the race. I told Jeff and he told his people. They didn't believe me. They thought I banked the bet hoping they would lose. That night, Jeff came to my house and pulled his gun on me. He told me in no uncertain terms to never let that happen again. That's when I realized this was not for fun.

It was a great day when Charlie got paid for renovating the racetrack. It was big money. He gave me credit for my part and asked me what I wanted as a bonus. I told him I wanted a 450SL Mercedes convertible. That would be quite a dream car. Charlie then offered to take me to the Clearwater resort on the west coast of Florida. It was a fancy country club and he was a member. There was a good Mercedes dealership in Miami, so we decided to go there, get my brand new shiny bonus, drive to Clearwater to celebrate and then I'd drive myself back the next day. Charlie may have wanted this to be his special moment - after all, I had been dodging his flirtations for a long time - but I earned this bonus and had no intention of showing gratitude with my loins this particular night, either.

We went to the dealer and I picked out a beautiful silver one-year-old 450SL. It was a sight to behold - both the car itself and watching Charlie pay in full with cash. The dealer had me sign all the paperwork, put the car in my name and I drove over to the Clearwater Resort in style.

We had a lovely dinner that night and I toasted a glass of wine while Charlie toasted his fourth glass of scotch. Halfway through dinner, I felt funny - very drunk or ill or something. Half a glass of expensive wine wouldn't make me feel that woozy, but I could barely sit up. I wanted to go upstairs and lie down. Charlie quickly paid the check and left.

To my surprise, we had only one room, but with two beds. I was about to lose consciousness, so instead of protesting for a separate room I fell into a separate bed and passed out.

I was woken by the gross weight of his heavy, naked body reeking of scotch and cigarettes wriggling on top of me. I tried to fight him off but was too drunk from whatever was in the wine. I was tossing and squirming around trying to get the beast off of me. My struggling underneath him made him so excited he came before he penetrated me. Thank God. I was so disgusted.

Charlie was happy. He went to his bed and fell asleep. In shock and unable to move, I lay there waiting for the effect to wear off. I was repulsed every time I recalled what had happened that night, but I was mostly mad at myself. What did I expect? I had been suggesting all along that when the time was right I was willing to play. Oh god. I guess he got tired of waiting and created his own play date. What was I thinking?

By morning, he was very pleased with himself and began behaving as if we were a couple. I sat through breakfast unable to look at the contented pig. I was revolted and ashamed. I told him what he did to me and that I was going home.

When I got back I didn't know what to do. I was afraid to tell anyone about it. I knew I'd been foolish and more than aware he was a lecherous boss but it had gotten out of control and I didn't want to go back to the office ever again. I wanted out. I could never look at him again.

I worried about the bills I had incurred from my lavish lifestyle. I figured if I needed money to hold me over I could always sell the car.

Monday morning I got a call from the Mercedes dealer telling me there was a recall on the steering and I needed to bring the car in. We made an appointment for Tuesday morning. When I arrived at the dealership, they told me to leave it there overnight and pick it up Wednesday. I called Mom and got a ride home.

When I returned on Wednesday afternoon I went to the service department and no one knew anything about the car. There was no record of me or the car or even the sales transaction. I was stunned. I had made the mistake of leaving the temporary tag info in the car and the rest of the paperwork was in Charlie's office, so I had no evidence. I kept repeating, "No, you have to know where it is. It's the silver 450SL. I was just here the other day." They looked at one another as if I was speaking another language and shrugged their shoulders.

Charlie had the dealer trick me into returning the car so he could get his money back since I ended our "relationship".

He kept calling me to come back, but there was no way that was going to happen. I'd rather starve. My construction company wouldn't help support me because I couldn't pull permits without Charlie's license. I had to give it all up as I was not about to be beholden to a devious, deceitful pervert. So, once again everything I worked hard for was gone. I regretted that having that smelly fat man on top of me, after he had drugged me, was all for nothing. I shuttered.

Jeff was right there to pick up the pieces. I went seamlessly back to making money at the track during the day and clubbing at night with Mom. I had grown into my big brown eyes, and my eighteen-year-old hot body, barely covered in trendy, expensive clothes, drew men to me like a magnet. I was no longer a clone of Betty but a different, more exotic version. I knew I was getting the looks, but I liked to play hard to get.

It didn't take long before my mother became possessive of me. She wanted me to go out with her exclusively and spend my money only on her. She behaved like she and I were dating. If I went out with other friends she would repeat over and over, "They don't really like you. They only want you for your money." She figured if I was buying any meals or gifts they should only be for her since she brought me in this world. She did her best to run off any potential friends.

One night I was with some friends in a club in Fort Lauderdale ordering bottles of Dom Perignon, dancing and enjoying this new life of extravagance when I met a handsome man named Robert. He was in the Champagne room looking over at me and holding his glass up in a toast. I smiled a little teasing smile and then ignored him. He sent his bodyguard over with a bottle of Dom and asked if I would join him for dinner the next evening. I accepted.

Robert owned an elite nightclub in Miami. He was not very tall but he had the cutest face with big brown eyes. When he spoke the whole place would turn around. He looked so important with his thousand dollar custom suits and two thousand dollar shoes. Robert's Rolex cost as much as my mother's house. He drove a Rolls Royce with the first car phone. I was impressed.

Robert took me to his club for dinner. There were hundreds of people lined up to get in the club and we walked past the crowd to his private entrance. The place looked like a palace complete with expensive chandeliers, a wine cellar and marble floors. He made me feel like a princess. Waiters would fall all over me to satisfy my every need.

We started dating exclusively. I went to his club every night and we partied like there was no tomorrow. It was quite a scene with cocaine, beautiful women, hot music and lots of sex. Everyone told me he was part of the Columbian drug cartel. I knew it was dangerous, but I didn't care.

Robert was into alternative sex and I was into Robert. I'd stay with him over the weekend and he would bring home pretty girls for a night of wild fun. I wasn't thrilled about sharing him, but he wanted multiple partners and I went along with it to make him happy. The night would turn into any man's fantasy with beautiful women doing everything asked of them. The women were very generous to me and I tried to get turned on, but it just wasn't for me. I didn't get upset or anything - I was a bit of a bohemian myself, but sex with women was not my thing. Sex with Robert was.

We had been dating for about six months when I showed up at the club and found him in his office with another woman. That just wasn't going to work for me, so I went straight to his house and picked up all my things.

About a week later, Robert got arrested for drug trafficking. When he got out on bail I called him to see if he was all right. He said he missed me and asked me to come over. I hesitated. I still had feelings for him, but knew I couldn't handle his lifestyle. I wanted to see him one more time, though - just for closure. I don't like loose ends. We made plans for me to come the following weekend. I was looking forward to it I was just hoping that I didn't fall for his cute self again.

The next day I heard on the evening news that there had been a double murder. It was Robert and the new girlfriend. Apparently, she went out to walk the dog in the early morning. The bodyguard was in front and she had slipped out the back. A gunman grabbed her and made her bring him to where Robert was sleeping. He then put fifteen bullets into Robert's body and five into her head.

That could easily have been me. Lucky I was playing hard to get.

Chapter 10
LA

After that big eye-opener, I went back home to figure out what I was going to do next. I was still living with Mom and she was not pleased with the situation. The social security payments had stopped coming and she wasn't about to let me live there for free. I needed to get away from her. I was only sleeping there because it was convenient. She was still working nights and I was out all the time, but she demanded that I give her money or get out. I decided to get out. I went to see my buddy Jeff at the track to see what was going on hoping I could still run numbers if I get in a pinch.

Jeff suggested that I go to LA for a week and check things out. He said that it was easy to find jobs there and he'd set me up with some people he knew. He had planned on going the next day so he told me to meet him there a few days later. He generously offered to pay my expenses. Who could pass that up? Since Jeff was leaving right away, he asked if I didn't mind taking an extra bag for him, as he was already over the limit.

After Robert, I needed a fresh start. I also needed to get away from my nagging mother.

When I arrived, a stranger came up to me and said he was a friend of Jeff's. I was a little nervous since I had no way of knowing he was telling the truth. As usual, I threw caution to the wind and took the ride. The second we got into his car, he opened up Jeff's bag. It was filled with little white pills. I later found out they were Quaaludes and I was the mule. I wasn't thrilled that I had been conned, but since I made some spending money I let it go.

I loved it in LA. Jeff took me around Hollywood and all the glamorous places. He knew everybody. He was friends with Dennis Cole, Jacqueline Smith's husband, and Chuck Norris. I met directors and movie stars - all the "beautiful people" of Los Angeles. Jeff was very popular there. I figured he must have been their supplier. I didn't ask questions. It's better not to ask questions.

He introduced me to a woman my age named Toni. She was the daughter of one of his friends from the track. Toni was in the movie business. I wasn't exactly sure what that meant, but it sounded exciting. She was beautiful with her long dark hair and big brown eyes. Right away people thought we were sisters. We instantly became friends.

I didn't have much money then, but you would never know it. I still had an amazing wardrobe along with thousands of dollars worth of jewelry - gifts from good old Charlie. I fit right in at the parties and premieres.

Toni, along with her cousin Lori, and some other friends were looking to rent a big house and asked if I would like to live there and help spilt the rent. This seemed like the perfect answer to a fresh start and I happily agreed.

Needing money, I thought about Jeff's offer to do another mule run. Since I needed to go back to Florida to get my things, I figured why not? So he set me up to do one more round trip. I left my suitcase with Lori and Toni, took a couple of big ones that Jeff's "friend" gave me and flew home. I gathered all the things I needed for California, plus a few more suitcases and when I arrived back in LA, the same man picked me up and inspected the bags. He then paid me a nice chunk of money and dropped me off at my new house. Easy.

Toni, Lori and Lindy were all sort of in the film business - "sort of" being the operative word. We always had budding celebrities at our house - people like Scott Baio, Tony and Matt Danza, Kenny G and Randy

Jackson. They were not quite stars yet, but they had promise.

I needed to find a job. I was clear that I didn't want to be a mule for income so I applied at a telemarketing company and got the job right away. All I had to do was call various office managers of certain companies that used products for photocopying machines. I got a commission on every sale. With my early training in candy sales, I kicked ass and was outselling everyone.

I got this idea to offer a free clock radio to the person in charge of ordering the supplies at various offices. It worked every time. I scored heavily. Hell, they weren't the ones footing the bill, so whether or not their company needed ink, they ordered. I was relieved to be back making good money again.

I worked all day and partied all night - just like in Florida. This time I was dating celebrities and going to the Playboy Mansion. Life was great, I was nineteen and nothing was stopping me.

At work, I was brimming with all kinds of good ideas about how our company could make more money so I asked to talk to the owner. She was a strange, skinny woman with extra large boobs. Between leather skin, weathered hair and the hollow look one gets when they are missing fat pads in the cheeks, she appeared to have washed up from one too many parties in her life. She had a snippy personality too, which only added to her unattractiveness. Maybe it wasn't fair to judge her. After all, my nights were filled with the beautiful people so, who wouldn't look plain in comparison? Didn't matter anyway, as she didn't want to take a meeting with me. I was just a salesperson not worth her time.

Too bad for her.

Jeff asked me to do another mule run. I declined as I was having some regrets about doing all that illegal stuff. I figured I would only do it in an emergency. I was quite pleased with my decision when Jeff called me and told me the man who picked me up at the airport when I was the mule was found shot dead in his house. I stood there frozen. Another lucky escape.

Chapter 11
TRUST ISSUES

One night I was going to a very fancy private party for the LA Lakers. One of my roommates had some kind of relationship with Jerry Buss and I was set up with his son. He was cute but a little shy and timid - not the powerhouse his dad was. I wanted to look impressive, so I went to my safe and took out all the valuable jewelry that Charlie had given me. I must have looked a little like I was going to the Oscars with all the diamonds I was flashing. I had them on every finger and wore a lavish necklace that sparkled like nobody's business.

The party was amazing. It was for the Lakers and their "close friends" after they won the championship. Every celebrity in Hollywood seemed to be close to someone on the team. The party was crawling with Playboy bunnies, calendar girls and Chippendale boys. I held my own in my Vera Wang dress and sparkly jewelry. Matty Danza and Jerry Buss' son were fighting over me. At about 4am after having the most amazing time that was enough ego boosting for me so I headed back to my house.

I got home very late and very loaded, stripped down to my underwear and went right to sleep. The next morning I flew out of bed, worried that I might be late for work. That would have been unacceptable. Not for my boss hag, but for my own ethics. I was never late - it was something ingrained in me by my mother. Once at work, I remembered that I never put my jewelry back into the safe. It made me a little nervous but I let it go because my roommates were around all day and we lived in a very upscale neighborhood.

After a long day making hundreds of calls while nursing a bit of a hangover, I arrived home to find everything gone - my clothes, my jewelry, even my underwear. I had nothing left - nothing but the clothes on my back. I was the *only* one of the five girls in the house who was missing anything and I was missing EVERYTHING. The police came but there was nothing they could do. They had no leads.

Lucky, I had enough money to buy a plane ticket to go home. I was grateful for the clothes I had stored at my mom's house.

My mother wouldn't take me back unless I had rent money up front, so I called a friend who had just gotten married and moved to a bigger place. I rented his townhouse. I didn't know how I was going to pay him but I was sure I could figure that out later.

I had an ongoing and atypical relationship with "trust". Though clearly I had no reason to trust others, I trusted myself - implicitly. I identified with the cat that landed on her feet no matter how far she fell. When I got back to Florida I made myself a promise that I would be a millionaire before I reached twenty, and though I had barely one year to go, I was convinced I could do it. Even though I was not sure how I was going to pay my first month's rent, I came back with an abundance of ideas on how I'd support myself.

I had learned quite a lot about telemarketing while I was in California and saw that Florida was way behind the times. Telemarketing was hardly exploited in the early eighties so I knew exactly how I was going to make good on that promise I made to myself.

I bought a paper and found some office space to rent. A man named Ron owned an office building that was partially empty. Of course I had nothing for a down payment, but I did have a great idea. Using my candy sales persona, I let Ron in on my plans. To prove to him the timing was right, I picked up his phone and cold called some random person out of the Yellow Pages, offered them a free gift and made my first sale. Ron was impressed and he decided to be my partner. Since I didn't have anything to lose, I went ahead and ordered fifteen desks and phone lines, put an ad in the paper, hired six sales people and trained them - all in about three week's time. I had done some of the product ordering when I was working in LA, so I knew where to get the same product. We started selling before we had to pay for our first order. Within a month we were going like gangbusters.

I worked my ass of all day, but didn't forget to party at night. This time I had attitude. I had been with celebrities and knew some key people in LA, so my new Florida entourage was in awe. We went to a different "A" party every night. I was behaving as though I was already a millionaire.

My work was impeccable. I kept an eye on the employees, giving them incentive to sell their little asses off. Within three months, we had paid Ron back his investment and were making a killing.

One Monday, I got to the office early as usual and when I put my key in the door it would not open. I couldn't understand why. Ron came outside and said, "We no longer need your services."

"What the hell are you talking about, Ron? This is *my* business."

He stared at me for a few unnerving seconds and then spoke with entitlement, "This is my place, Gigi. I am the sole owner of this business. I legally own it and I am firing one of my employees." He had not blinked. "That would be you."

"What the fuck are you talking about? This was *my* idea. *I* found the employees. *I* ordered the product. *I* got this thing off the ground. *You* know it and *I* know it. Am I going to have to see you in court?"

"If you wish." He was such a cold bastard. "Just don't forget to bring proof."

He had me there.

I still had three quarters of a year left to make my millions, so I moved on.

While I was in LA, I had gained more confidence about myself and the way I looked, so my next thought was to try to be the swimsuit model for the Miami Beach Department of Tourism. It wouldn't make me millions, but I thought it could lead me to some of the influential business people who would, in turn, take me seriously once they got to know me. My idea was to get out and meet as many people as I could - and it wouldn't hurt to be "the representation of Miami Beach."

I got it! They wanted to do a photo shoot a week from Tuesday, which gave me ten days to die of anticipation.

That Thursday I was invited to go down to the Coconut Grove with my friend Tina. It was perfect - we could hobnob with the Floridian socialites and up my chances to meet even more people who might get me to my goal.

On the drive down there I started feeling sick, like food poisoning or something. We went to a friend's house and I lay on the couch hoping it would subside. I was having terrible pains and could not breathe. It was getting so bad Tina had to take me to the hospital. After running a few tests, the doctor announced that my appendix had ruptured and I was going to die if he didn't quickly remove it. I told him I had a modeling contract where I had to show off my perfect belly in a swimsuit. He must have thought I was joking. I can assume he was thinking, "Let's see, should I save this young woman's life or keep her body perfect for a small swimsuit? Cut? No cut? I just don't know what to do."

He promised me he would make a tiny incision and no one would ever see it. As I was signing the papers he had shoved in my face, he promised I would back in a week. Could I trust him? I didn't know what to do, but I was so sick I just wanted it out. I reluctantly signed and they took me away.

After surgery, I spent the following four days in the hospital blowing up balloons to make sure my lungs were working properly. Once everything seemed to be in working order, Tina picked me up to finish recuperating back at my townhouse. My place was unfurnished and the bedroom was upstairs. There was no way I could climb two, let alone ten, stairs so Tina brought down my blankets and I slept on the floor of my empty living room. I was reminded of those first years when my mom took us away from Dad.

I had no idea how big the scar was or what shape my body was in because I was wrapped up like a mummy. I just prayed he did as little damage as possible. Those swimsuits were quite tiny. I gave myself two days to heal and then the bandages had to come off.

I was filled with anxiety when we arrived at the doctor's office. As he began to unravel the bandages, I could see a huge black and burgundy snake slithering its way from three inches *above* my bellybutton down to where my appendix used to live. There had to be thirty staples holding my hacked body together. I was in shock. Staring down at what looked like a bloody zipper I asked, "Why did you cut me that way? You said it would be a small incision under my bikini line!"

Hot tears were set free as he explained that he had decided to do exploratory surgery since he wasn't exactly sure what was wrong. I chastised him saying that it was not what I had expected. I asked him who did he think was going to hire me now? He told me to return in two weeks to remove the stitches.

I went home to lick my wounds like a beaten dog without a cone. I called the director of tourism and thanked him for the opportunity then told him about my gruesome journey. I readily admitted that I didn't think he would want me anymore. He thanked me for the call and wished me good luck.

I sat there brooding. Then I remembered that I usually *did* have good luck. After all, how many deaths had I escaped already? Three? Four? I thought about the cat again and how I still had about four months left to reach my goal.

While I was waiting to have my freaky stitches removed, I restlessly went to see if Jeff could get me some work. Jeff always had work for me. He never let me down. Sometimes I think we were made for each other - he made money with me and I made money with him. So I simply picked up where I left off running numbers. I planned to do that just long enough to get some money to go back into telemarketing.

Meanwhile, I went back to my partying ways at night. It didn't take long to whip my body back in shape. I covered my big ole scar with beautiful, expensive clothes and went to Fort Lauderdale with my friend Robin. She was the girlfriend of a wealthy drug dealer. She and I both chose not to do drugs, but we both loved to be around the excitement. Robin was a real beauty with long, brown hair, big eyes and the biggest cheekbones. She was every man's dream but she was off limits. We loved to go out and drink our Dom and drive the men crazy.

After a day of making bets for other people and getting a nice bit of cash for myself, Robin and I would go out to this lavish club in Fort Lauderdale and tease the men. That's where we met the sons of rich Arabs. They owned a lot of fancy racehorses and lived at the Diplomat Hotel. They rented half the place and threw wild parties after the club hours. I had heard that some of the most elite and wealthy people from all over the world went to after hour parties.

One night Robin invited me to go to one after the club. I was disappointed because I had other plans I could not break. I was going to the Diplomat to party with other friends. Lady luck was indeed on my side because that night there was a drug bust and they arrested everyone including Robin.

I had also made friends with a man named Tony who was the hairdresser for the Sheik's wife. After Robin was busted in a drug sting, he offered to help her get out of jail. Tony was having immigration problems himself. He was from Lebanon and he was about to be deported unless he was married. He asked me if I could marry him to help his beloved Robin. She and I were not *that* good of friends - we just liked to hang out during that time. Why should I marry a Lebanese man who was lovesick over someone I barely knew? I have no good answer for that, but I did it. I went to the courthouse and married Tony.

Tony was able to stay while the paperwork was in process and he somehow got Robin out of jail. What he didn't realize was that there was a whole line of hungry men who were also smitten with her beauty and my new husband was not very high up on the list. Shocked and brokenhearted, he disappeared. There I was stuck in a marriage with a man from Lebanon with no clue as to his whereabouts.

With my days at the track to keep me going, I was happy with my new name. It had a nice ring. I felt like a new person. Carrying my father's name had bothered me since he hadn't cared about me except maybe for one day. One day does not make a father, so in the end I was happy to be Gigi Nassar.

My night life was interesting as ever. I met a man named Sammy who became my best friend. I might have had a small crush on him at first but he had so many girlfriends it was better to be friends. We started hanging out at Turnberry Island on Thursday nights, the Cricket Club on Fridays; Regina's on Saturdays - on Sundays our faces were in the Grove as the "it" couple. These were the most popular and most elite clubs in Florida. People like Whitney Houston, Pat Benatar and James Caan frequented Turnberry, and Sammy and I were regulars alongside the privileged. We were hot. No one did anything without us.

One day I was walking on the beach in Hollywood when someone handed me a paper. I saw this offer to visit the first hotel in Florida that was going to go timeshare. Now that I had given myself one more year to become a wealthy twenty-one-year-old I could definitely see possibilities. The timeshare in Florida was a great idea, but the marketing part was slow and outdated. One night at Turnberry, I noticed an older man who had been coming in every Thursday with an entourage of beautiful young girls. I knew they could not all be his daughters, so I asked around. His name was Ike and all those young, dressed-to-kill, model types were his girlfriends. He walked around as if he was the Hugh Heffner of Florida.

I was enormously curious to know what he did to get so rich so I walked right up to Ike and introduced myself. He was immediately impressed and invited me over to his place the next day. I was unsure of his intentions, but my curiosity and daring nature were in charge so I went.

Ike had the whole penthouse floor. I knocked on the door and it opened electronically. It looked like a palace with all the mirrors and gold faucets and incredible décor. He proudly gave me a tour. Though it was not The Playboy Mansion and he was hardly Hugh Heffner, I was impressed. The girls had their own apartments. Three to four extremely young women occupied each room. In all, there were about ten stunning women - five of which looked under age. I wanted to know what he did for a living.

We talked for quite a while, but it was hard to keep his attention away from my breasts and on the meat and potatoes of his business world. He told me he owned a hotel in Hollywood that was going timeshare. Surprised, I pulled out the paper I had gotten on the beach and asked if that was the one. He replied that it was, in fact, the one. I begged for the opportunity to do some marketing for him. I told him about my telemarketing idea, and how I had some great ideas for him - like how I would offer the public a free stay there and then, when he had a captive audience, he could do his sales speech. He was impressed that I had brains *and* boobs. He was not used to that.

He loved my ideas and told me to go ahead and begin. He offered me a commission for every person who showed up - whether or not they bought anything. I was so excited and knew I was on target to become rich. The only problem was that I had no start up money. I had no office, no sales people, and no telephones. I didn't tell Ike this as he was too impressed with my business-like qualities. Besides, my head was filled with great ideas that would surely make me, and everyone around me, rich.

I went back to the man I met on the beach who gave me the paper about the timeshare. Turned out his name was Bill and he was a friend of a friend of my mother's. I told him I met the owner of the hotel and that he gave me a contract to bring people to the hotel. I shared all my ideas with him. He loved them. We made a plan. Though he didn't have much money, it was just enough.

I was a little more cautious this time. I was quite aware I needed to be the one that rented the place. I went to Jeff and asked to borrow ten thousand dollars.

Jeff went to the other side of the fence and got me my money. Understandably, I had to pay it back with interest. I reminded him I knew the drill. Within a week we were in business.

Bill was charming and handsome, tall and thin, sporting a five o'clock shadow with amazing blue eyes. I could hardly contain my crush on him but I did. He was older and he was married to my mom's friend. That didn't stop the little flirtatious moments I enjoyed so much, but that's where it ended.

Business was booming and Ike could not have been happier. My marketing plan was working. We called on people and offered a three-day, two-night vacation for eighty-nine dollars. That covered the cost of our overhead. If they showed up, Ike paid us two hundred dollars, and if they bought a timeshare we made a thousand dollars. It was great.

For fun I loved hanging out with Ike and the girls. I was the only one with a job. I didn't live there, but sometimes I would stay with one of the girls. Usually it was this one named Dallas. I enjoyed watching all the drama that comes with that size of harem. Girls were jealous of one another. They would get catty or whiny. Every night a different girl would get her chance to sleep with Ike. They fought over him. I could not tell if he was a great lover or had a big package or if they were just excited because the one who slept with Ike was invited to go shopping the next day.

Dallas, one of Ike's girlfriends, was a real beauty at barely seventeen. One day her mom just dropped her off with Ike so she could have a chance at a better life. To me he was a chauvinist, controlling, creepy pedophile - not a place I would put my daughter.

He would make passes at me but I came off as the smart business girl and made him think he would have to work a little harder for me. All the girls eventually came to trust me and wanted to get away from Ike. Sometimes, I would hide them at my house. I felt bad for Dallas. She was so innocent. I wanted to help her. Ike was crazy about her but I wanted to protect her without jeopardizing my future business with him. I wanted to give her the message her mother should have; that she could live a life other than as a sex slave for Ike and a few trinkets.

One Monday I went to Bill's office to have a meeting to organize our finances. I got there in the early afternoon, knocked on the door and he invited me in. The room was dark. I could barely make out the bottle of wine, two glasses and some cocaine. I was quite shocked. He was stoned. He got up and walked toward me. He had a strange look on his face. I felt uncomfortable and he grabbed me, threw me against the wall and started kissing me. That's not at all what I expected. His embrace was anything but tender. I told him I was interested in him, but not as a married man. I told him that when he was man enough to take care of that little problem, I would be his. So, off I went.

That week Bill didn't show up, so I ran the office by myself. That was fine with me. I didn't want to see him. Sales were good that week and everyone was happy.

After another wild weekend of partying between Turnberry and the Cricket Club, before I knew it Monday showed up and it was time for work. I arrived at the office and opened the door to an empty place. There was nothing - no furniture, no employees - not even the sound of the phone ringing as it always had. I called one of the employees at home. She said that Bill told her that the company moved and everyone was to report to the new office. He had also deceived the phone company, telling them we moved and he changed the name on the account. I couldn't believe I was duped again.

I had just put another slime ball in business.

I never showed my hand with Ike. I let him think that I was an infallible businesswoman. The truth was I had not only been ripped off and was without a company, but this time I owed Jeff ten thousand dollars. That was a big problem. I went to Jeff right away hoping that he would go find Bill, get the money and punish him for what he did to me.

Later that night Jeff came to my house.

"Did you get the money from Bill?" I asked hoping it was all over.

"I didn't lend the 10K to fuckin Bill," he reminded me. "I lent it to you. With interest."

"I don't have it. I don't have anything," I responded. "But don't worry. You know I always land on my feet, Jeff. I'll get it to you. Just give me a little time, that's all. We're cool."

He stepped a little closer to me. It felt uncomfortable.

I said with irritation, "Get it from Bill if you want it *now*. Otherwise, give me a minute to figure it out, okay?"

He cocked his head slightly as if he didn't quite hear me, but before I had a chance to repeat myself he threw a powerful punch to my face, knocked me to the floor, kicked me in the belly and told me I had one week to get him his fucking money.

Lying in extreme pain, I could not believe what had just happened. After everything that Jeff and I had been through, how could he do this to me? Why wouldn't he help me go get Bill? I never understood this, but it was clear I needed to find ten thousand fast.

I reluctantly went to Ike, I told him what happened and that I needed to borrow twenty thousand dollars. I didn't tell him anything about Jeff - just that I needed the money to open another office. He gave it to me after I showed him my plan with no partners! I told him to keep the commissions until I paid the loan back. Ten thousand was for Jeff and the rest was enough for me to start again.

I went to the track and gave Jeff the money. I never talked to him again.

I was very sad to end our relationship. He was the only one who I could talk to about anything. We made so much money together.

I would never forgive him for hitting me.

I found a warehouse to rent right away. It was perfect and cheap and the landlord, whose name was Avi, he was so cute. He was an electrical contractor and shared the downstairs offices with a general contractor and an accountant.

I quickly got phones, desks, everything I needed together. Ike agreed that he would not supply anything to that creep Bill, so I called the employees that had abandoned me and offered them more money. They came right back. I knew I needed to sell more than vacations since I had such a big debt, so I added selling photocopy products again. I put my clubbing on hold and sold the office products by day and vacations by night. My office was going fourteen hours a day.

Within two months, Ike was completely paid back. Between his commissions and my office supply income, I was back on track but it was time to make some real money. There were millions waiting to be made... and horses waiting to be bought.

No time to lose.

Chapter 12
AVI

My new landlord, Avi, was about thirteen years older than me and had a ten-year-old daughter who stayed with him every other weekend. He was quite sexy and I couldn't help but flirt with him every time I went to the downstairs offices. Avi returned the favor, but he was dating someone - a woman more his age, so we just kept it to a flirt. A strong, intensely entertaining flirt.

Down the hall from Avi was John, who owned the construction company. John was attracted to me and while John flirted with me, I flirted with Avi. It's a wonder any of us got work done. Actually, that part we did well. We were all thriving. Avi was an electrical engineer but was a savvy business man who owned a lot of real estate and was a very tough Israeli always acting like a sergeant in the army that was so sexy to me. John was kind of a wimp a push over kind of reminded me of Albert from school.

A lot of Ike's girls would come over to my place, especially Dallas. She and I were building a strong friendship. I took her to the racetrack with me and we enjoyed each other's company. I felt sorry for the girls. The girls were sex slaves to Ike. I tried to coach them and give them jobs in my telemarketing office but they didn't want that kind of hard work. They preferred lying on their backs for rich men and then going shopping afterward.

An older, rich, married friend named Joey who I knew from the track took an interest in Dallas and invited us to dinner. We went to the most upscale restaurant in Miami. I used to go there with Robert before he was murdered, and we would drink Chateau Lafitte, which was at least a thousand dollars a bottle.

Joey ordered the same wine. He had brought a friend name Lewis as a date for me. I was not that impressed with either of them since they both had wives waiting for them at home.

After a fun-filled evening and expensive wine for me and cocaine for Dallas, the two of us stumbled home to my house and fell asleep around three in the morning. There turned out to be consequences. Dallas had broken the Ike Rule - Ike girls were never allowed to go out without Ike, and they were *always* supposed to come home to Ike. He was not happy that I took his little girl from his harem. He abruptly ended his relationship with the both of us. That was fine with me. I had had enough with his rules and exploitation of young girls. Sure I needed the commissions, but there were always other ways to make money.

Dallas moved in with me and became Joey's mistress. Joey and his wife lived at Turnberry. Both Turnberry Island and The Cricket Club had posh condos above the chic nightclub and restaurant. Dallas would party with him all night and sleep all day. He would give her gobs of cash. I would work my ass off for fourteen hours every day and she still had more money than me. It was a good situation for Joey to have Dallas at my place so he generously paid her share of the rent, which I appreciated.

I always thought Dallas was wasting her talent. She should have been a model. She looked a little like a teenage Brooke Shields with luxurious long, blonde hair and very nice sized breasts. One time she and I went to the Playboy Club for dinner. I knew the owner and thinking Dallas would be a great playboy bunny, I introduced them. Once he set eyes on the young beauty he had something else in mind. He wanted her for the Penthouse centerfold. She ended up with a twelve-page spread and became a Penthouse Pet. Dallas got a huge chunk of money which she blew it up her nose in less than a month. Not doing drugs myself I couldn't understand the waste in that but she didn't share my ambition of becoming a millionaire by the time I was twenty-one. Besides, she didn't have to worry - she still had Joey.

When the two of us would go for a wild night at Turnberry, we hung out with people like James Caan and Michael Jackson's brothers and other well-known entertainers. We were friends with the owner, which was a big deal. He had a huge yacht docked outside called The Monkey Business; all kinds of monkey business like mounds of coke for Dallas and wild sex and expensive champagne. That's where the celebrities went for fun. Like most men, the owner was crazy about Dallas so we partied all night on the boat.

That's where I met Tony. He had dirty blonde hair and olive green eyes and sported one of those George Michael five o'clock shadows. He was the coolest guy in the club. We would dance and drink shots of melon balls all night. I was from the same side of the street as him and had a bit of a crush on him but didn't let on. He liked me because I didn't need or want anything from him.

People would admire Dallas and me, but I hated it when they would say, "Dallas, you're so beautiful. And Gigi ------ you're so smart!" It wasn't like I was plain or unattractive. I had my mother's beauty and had no problem attracting men but next to that seventeen-year-old dazzling little sex creature I paled by comparison. It was like they were mesmerized. Then at a certain point realized there was another entity standing right there so they quickly had to add on something - anything. "...And Gigi, you are so *smart*" were about all the words they had left. At the end of the day, though, I was glad to be smart. I knew how to earn money and even though it was not as much as Dallas, or any of Ike's girls, made in twenty minutes, I could always figure out some clever and interesting new way of earning it. Being smart was much more reliable than looks and a nose for coke.

It was Avi that kept my attention at work. I was so infatuated by everything about him, especially his savvy business ways. He was just sexy! He was of the Jewish faith and observed the Sabbath. Though I was technically Jewish by birth, I thought it might be good for me to try a little religion and would attend Shabbat dinner at his home.

Avi and I continued our flirting until one day he asked me out on a real date. I questioned what happened to the girlfriend and he told me that it was over and he was available. I was so excited. I got all dressed up and we went to an Israeli restaurant that was kosher.

After dinner, he took me back to his house and threw me on the bed with a kind of passion I had never experienced. It was a most amazing night. I had been with other men and sex had been good but it was different with Avi. One touch and I melted. I became completely submissive and did anything and everything with him.

I was crazy about him, but he kept saying I was too young for him to be serious. He would remind me that I was only ten years older than his daughter; we continued our wild and exciting affair anyway. I spent the night with him most nights while Dallas occupied my house.

Meanwhile John, the construction guy in the office building, was getting weird on me. I guess in the beginning I was innocently flirting with him - but I was flirting with everyone at that time. I never dated him, though. We were just friends. My eyes were always on Avi. Once Avi and I started dating, I caught John following me and waiting outside my house when I would come home from a night partying. It was unnerving.

Avi got a contract in Jamaica importing heavy equipment. The Israelis were building a fish farm with the Jamaican government. He invited me to come with him and we flew down there to get all the specs. I wanted to help Avi with my connections I had from my construction business. The Israelis were geniuses. They built this farm in the middle of nowhere, bred and raised the fish for consumption, and then exported them all over the world. There were hundreds of acres with thousands of Jamaican men and women working.

When we arrived at the camp we were treated like royalty. The Jamaicans were proud of their service. There were different groups of workers at the farm, but at lunch everyone ate in the cantina. We were served first, and then all the men got in line for the food that was served by the women. After all the men were happy the women finally got to eat. I could not understand that method and it drove me crazy.

Working and traveling with Avi made it seem like we were a couple. And even though he would remind me now and again that I was too young for him, he did not behave that way in bed.

We arrived back home and I went to what, by comparison, seemed like a boring company. But it still put butter on my bread. After losing Ike's contract, I had subleased the phone room at night and I ran my crew selling photocopy supplies during the day. They paid me enough to cover all my expenses, so whatever I sold, excluding product, was profit.

I spent most of my days finding equipment and working the prices for Avi's company. I made a commission on everything we bought and sold. My life was great. My love for Avi was growing. I knew he loved me, but was afraid of my intentions. He thought I was still the party girl. I think Avi thought I was like Dallas who had a wild sex life. She wasn't loyal to anyone, not even herself. I had never cheated in any relationship ever so I couldn't understand why he didn't trust me.

Spending more time in Avi's office downstairs with my equipment purchases, only served to increase John's obsession with me. My relationship with Avi was still quiet and that made my job of controlling John much harder because he thought I was single and still had a chance with me. The fun stopped when I would see him lurking around at night.

One night I had planned to cook Avi a nice kosher dinner. I was head-over-heels in love at this point. It was my first time cooking for him so I shopped at the kosher market where I scored a recipe or two from the other patrons. I went back to his house to create while Avi was playing racket ball.

While the meal was simmering, I decided to really show off my domestic prowess by doing his laundry. I turned down the flame on the chicken and gathered his clothes. The washer and dryer were in the garage. I went out with my full load and started to place the laundry in the washer when I heard a loud noise. It shook the house slightly. Then there was another one, then another one. I quickly ran inside and the noise stopped. Maybe it was a firecracker or a car backfiring or something. I could only hope.

Twenty minutes later, I went out to put the clothes into the dryer and as I walked passed Avi's beautiful Mercedes, I noticed the windshield had a big hole in it. I was absolutely sure that it had not been there before. Avi was going to kill me. Somehow I broke his car doing laundry. How was that possible? Did the vibration from the washing machine knock something over? I went back into the house and noticed there were holes in the walls!

Avi pulled in the driveway and came in through the garage. The first thing he saw was the car. I met him at the door and told him I didn't know what happened but I had heard the noise.

We called the police. In the investigation they confirmed that someone had shot the car and the house. I didn't know if the bullets were for Avi or me. I told the police about John following me. They went to his house and found the shotgun in his car and arrested him.

I had no idea what kind of danger I had been in. What if he had hit his mark? Was I his target? How many times was I going to be in harm's way - and come out without a scratch? A much worse consequence had taken place, as Avi thought we should cool off. He didn't want me at his house anymore. Most of all, he was afraid for his daughter. I was heartbroken, but I understood (sort of). We tried to stop seeing each other, but it was difficult. We had something special and with this new restriction it was even more enticing - like forbidden fruit. He would come to my house every night. He could not break away from me.

We often went back to Jamaica. Business was booming there. My life was like a fairytale. We would go to this exotic place and work all day and eat Jerk chicken and smoke pot all night for weeks at a time. Then we'd head back to Florida where we promised to stay apart, only to be in even more exotic positions at night. Life sure was interesting.

There wasn't much for me to do when we were in Jamaica other than check in on the equipment. While Avi was busy with electrical work, I starting mingling with the employees; the women in particular. I learned they were slaves for the government by day and sex slaves by night. I thought it was crazy. These were the same conditions as Ike's girls, only with no shopping and not one perk. They didn't have birth control or condoms. They were made to spread their legs at anytime for anyone. Most of them had a few kids. It was so sad.

I started talking to them about women's rights and self-confidence and how to stand up for themselves. I was shocked to hear that there were groups of men in different power levels. The higher the power, the more women they had. They owned their women and the women had no benefits. This was not a law or a cult or religion. It was just something they got away with. The unfairness got to me so I told the women about other ways to protect themselves and gain power. By the second day, word had spread fast that the women were not going to have sex with the men unless they were treated with respect, and that they wanted to be paid in the same way as men. The men got so upset about their power being challenged they went crazy breaking things and refusing to work unless the women did what they wanted.

I didn't mean to disrupt a whole company of thousands of workers. I just wanted to give a little advice. It was getting dangerous so I was immediately escorted to the airport. The Israelis were not mad at me; they just were concerned for my safety and thought I shouldn't come back to the compound until it blew over.

Back in the telephone room in Florida, the photocopy supplies business was moving along. We weren't setting the world on fire, and the heavy equipment ordering started slowing down, so I decided to see what was going on with the tenants I had subleased the phone room to at night. I met one of the owners and hung around for a few nights watching. They were selling oil land leases in Alaska. They showed me all the land they owned and told me all about drilling for oil and all the successful customers they had. As usual, I got excited. I could see so much more they could do to get the most out of the job. They offered me an opportunity to train to sell their product. With my small education in real estate and securities, I could see where the training might come in handy. They were selling land for ten thousand dollars a pop, rather than the two hundred dollars worth of copy equipment, so the commission was enticing.

My relationship with Avi went up and down. One minute he would tell me I was not good for him; too young for him. He said we had to stop seeing each other. Next he would come over and have an amazing night of sex. It seemed like we could not get enough of each other.

When I was working in Avi's office organizing the heavy equipment, his secretary Trudy and I had become friends. One day we were out to lunch and I sensed she had something on her mind. I was a little afraid of what it might be, but I coaxed her into telling me anyway. She hesitated, which made me even more nervous. Finally, she said that Avi was getting married to his old girlfriend. I looked down and tried to keep the tears inside. She had to be lying. How could he be with someone else? He was constantly with me! I was incredibly shocked; stunned in disbelief. Trudy used to be the girlfriend's nanny and finally convinced me she was indeed telling the truth. I felt devastated as she went on to say they had been seeing each other for quite a while. I didn't hear anything else because my mind was spinning. How can this be? He loves me! Trudy begged me not to tell him she told me.

That night, brokenhearted, I went to see him as usual. I looked him in the eye and asked if there was something he wanted to tell me. He said that he loved me, but that I was too young for him and he needed stability. He said *she* was the one who could do that for him and that it was the best thing for his daughter. She was Jewish - not just in the inherited way - she was "kosher". She had two children in the same age group as his daughter. They both were friendly with other couples that were active in the temple. He was choosing a respectable life.

He told me he didn't want to stop seeing me. For the first time in my life I cut loose and cried. I was crushed, dazed and confused. I went home thinking maybe he was right - he already had a child; I was just twenty.

Going to the office was painful. Whenever I would see his car in the parking lot, I would be tempted to stop in his office on the way to mine and say hi - with the hope that once he saw me he would not be able to resist me. Instead, I wiped my tears and concentrated on selling oil leases. One of the owners was a handsome man named Billy. We flirted a little, but he just wasn't Avi.

I had completed my selling course and was ready to begin making those millions. Billy was a good distraction from my loss of Avi, and it wasn't long before he and I were getting cozy.

Avi was still coming over at night. I had no will power when it came to him and it seemed like we just couldn't keep our hands off each other even though he was still intent on getting married in two weeks. I kept thinking (hoping) that maybe he would change his mind.

When Trudy came back from being a bridesmaid at Avi's wedding and told me how wonderful it all was, I finally faced that it was over. It was true - he was gone. While he was on his honeymoon with his new wife, I was going crazy. The way he behaved around me did not fit with becoming a husband to someone else. I went back to the clubs to drown my sorrow in flirtatious men. I even gave Billy a try. He loved going out with me. After a few wild nights, we ended up at my house. He was so into me but the whole time we were having sex I was thinking of Avi. We continued our small affair without anyone at his office knowing. He wanted to keep it a secret. He said it would cause problems and jealousies at the office. I didn't care - I wasn't that into him.

Avi returned from his honeymoon three weeks later and came straight to my house. He grabbed me like he really missed me and was ready to pick up where we left off. I reluctantly sent him away but I was dying for him. I quickly went to see Billy to take my mind off him. Somehow, it just didn't do the trick.

While spending time in Billy's office watching the salespeople, something didn't seem right. I have a sixth sense about sales and something was odd about the content of their pitch. I began questioning as to whether or not there really was land or oil. I kept my suspicions to myself, but it affected my performance and I didn't make any sales. I knew one thing for sure... if I didn't believe in the product I couldn't talk anyone into it. I had to be enthusiastic about what I was selling and this was not working for me at all. I decided to abandon the Alaska sales and look toward something else to get me to my financial goal.

It became harder and harder for me to go to the office. Avi was downstairs and Billy was upstairs. The photocopy supply business was not making enough money and Billy's company was still paying enough on the sublease to cover rent but little more than the expenses. I was way short of the millions I had planned on.

Avi was still coming over to my house after work. I was trying to cut off the affair. I knew it was wrong but I didn't seem to have any self control when he came lusting after me. I remembered how I had been silently critical of Dallas being Joey's mistress and now I was no better. I hated that I was in love with him. It skewed my thinking. From my perspective it was as if I had him first and *she* took him away from *me*. Our affair was so intense. I knew it was going nowhere and guilt was creeping in about the wife. I don't know what he told her he was doing until ten or eleven every night, but I was becoming more and more unhappy. Finally, I couldn't take it anymore.

I had turned twenty-one and was not a millionaire. None of this was working. I needed to start fresh.

I made a decision to allow Billy's company to sublease straight to Avi and closed the photocopying business. I later found out that Billy was also married and that's why our affair was such a secret. I was finished with being powerless. I needed to take charge of my life.

I said adios to both men.

Chapter 13
FLOWERS

Turnberry Island was my very own professional headhunting office. While partying I met a man named Julio, who was in the wholesale flower business in Miami. He told me he needed help and by then I had quite a lot of experience and resources under my belt so I wanted to check it out. A very nice guy from Peru, he imported all the flowers you see in the supermarkets and the flower shops. His salespeople would call upon the wholesale stores regularly and see what they needed for that day. He had freezers where he stored all the beautiful flowers and greens that he imported from Columbia. When I would tell people I was going to work for a company importing greens from Columbia they would laugh with disbelief.

He hired me to do what I do best - use my phone skills and sell the hell out of flowers. I lit the place up! After only five days, I was selling more than the entire office did in a week. I wanted to take the sales all over the country. I figured we would pick up the flowers and greens at the airport by four in the morning (night) and we would start selling by seven AM. I explained that we could ship to any state FEDEX and they would have their goods the next day.

I was eager to go to work very early in the morning, soaking up all the data and figuring out how to improve my skills. This was the kind of thing that completely stimulated me. There was nothing better, or more fun, than to find a small business that thought and behaved like a small business and turn them into a huge business. Who needed cocaine - or Avi - when you had this kind of excitement?

Julio was focused on distribution and selling to the wholesalers. I was going to try to market to retailers. I wanted to sell direct and bypass the wholesalers, therefore making a higher profit.

I was not earning very much money to begin with so it was a good thing Dallas was still seeing Joey and he was paying her share of the rent. Dallas and I remained the queens of Turnberry. Between the action on the yacht Monkey Business and all the other rich guys she would spread her legs for, she was rolling in cocaine. I would go to all the parties, but with a very different goal. I loved to flirt and move myself up the social ladder. Everyone was so wild - the amount of money they smoked or put up their noses was unbelievable. I could hang with it, but I wasn't into throwing money away getting high.

After a night of partying on the Monkey Business, a bunch of us went back to a friend's condo above the club. Cindy had the penthouse apartment at the Cricket Club because she had a rich old married sugar daddy who took very good care of her. She was so pretty blond hair big blue eyes and the most perfect body. That night everyone, except me, was so high on cocaine they went crazy. Cindy and some other girls were so out of it they stood on her balcony about twenty or so floors high. Laughing and playing around, they thought they could fly and decided to climb up on the railing, I quickly pulled them to safety, kicked everyone out and put Cindy to bed and left.

I went to check on her the next evening. She was fine. She had no clue she was in danger in the first place. We went downstairs to the club and ran into Mark. He was the son of the club's owner and I had had my eye on him for months. Cindy was feeling fine and getting ready to do it all over again, so I switched my attention to Mark. We had a few drinks, started dancing and talking. He was Jewish. His father was very well connected and owned the famous restaurant where I would drink the thousand dollar bottles of wine. He told me he wanted to be a lawyer and not a business owner that his father wanted him to be. He said his father had made plans for him to marry an Arab woman and convert to Islam. He rebelled against his father's wishes and I became the lucky recipient.

We saw each other on and off for a few energizing months. We would do shots and I'd catch up on the new drama going on with his family. We had good sex and we liked being around each other.

I had not completely shaken Avi off. Though I tried several times to remain strong, Avi was still coming over. I didn't know how to get him out of my system and would compare every guy to him. Even Mark didn't hold a candle to Avi. I couldn't tell if it was just the fact that he was no longer "available" that made him so delicious or what.

One playful, sunny Saturday afternoon Dallas and I were walking on the beach when we met some guys from New York named Ted and Steve. Ted was immediately attracted to Dallas. And as soon as he pulled out the cocaine, Dallas was all his. Steve was a little loud and obnoxious, but he was entertaining. We were having a fun time when they invited us to go to New York for Ted's brother's wedding the following weekend. We agreed.

New York City blew me away. WOW - this was a place to be. Steve had a beautiful brownstone where he lived by himself, but his mother was not far away. In fact, she was just down the street. I was not used to the kind of guy that was sponsored by his parents. Dallas was busy with Ted getting high at the Ritz, so I was stuck staying with Steve at his place trying to have some privacy.

We spent Saturday shopping for the wedding and touring the city. The guys took us to buy dresses. Dallas was excited but I had reservations. I had never let myself be in a position where some guy - I hardly knew and was not sleeping with - would be buying me a dress. Charlie didn't count because I had worked for it. All I could think of was Ike - and his girls having sex with him in order to go shopping. I didn't want Steve to get that idea because I had no intention of thanking him in any way other than just saying it.

The wedding took place that evening. It was held at Tavern on the Green in Central Park. It was beautiful and magical. There was a moment when I became very sad I wanted to be with Avi but I quickly turned the page in my head. We ended up having a great time.

We all spent the next day hanging out and walking around interesting places in New York. I started noticing all the beautiful little flower shops that were on every corner. I went in to several and asked them where they got their flowers. Most said from the market on 7th downtown. I asked what they were paying for certain flowers. I got the sense they were paying retail. I told them I represented a grower in Colombia and proposed to sell them direct pointing out that I could save them forty percent. They were thrilled! The weekend was turning into something I could wrap my head around. Soon it was over and it was time to go home. Dallas was still high on everything while my head was organizing numbers.

Back at work on Monday, I told Julio about my weekend experience and asked him if he wanted to open a place in New York. I had it all thought out: we could ship straight to JFK, which would be cheaper than Miami customs. This got his attention. I quickly called the flower shop owners that I had met. One said he had a warehouse in Long Island City just five minutes outside the city. He said he would rent us the warehouse for exchange in product. Julio was ecstatic.

While it sounded great, I didn't have anything in New York. No place to live. No friends. I really would be starting over.

I then realized that might be the only way to get away from Avi.

Chapter 14
NEW YORK

I called Sammy, my best friend from Turnberry. It seemed like he knew everyone in the world. Sammy owned five hotels in Miami Beach. We were great friends and we would do anything for each other. He told me his friend Ronnie controlled New York and promised he'd call him. He assured me that Ronnie would hook me up with whatever I needed. So I grabbed Dallas and said, "Pack your bags, pretty girl! We're going back to New York to stay for a while!" She told Joey and he was happy because he was running out of places to hide her.

Just to be on the safe side I didn't give up my unfurnished Florida townhouse.

We flew to New York and headed to our new life. I knew this was a good idea when I saw the limo driver holding the sign that said "Gigi and Dallas". We quickly gathered our things and followed him to the limo. Ronnie was expecting us and, thanks to Sammy, he was giving us a place to stay. I was not sure what to expect as far as accommodations but with a limo driver taking us there, I had high hopes.

Driving through the city to our new adventure was thrilling. It was busy and lively with so many people walking in every different direction. Cars, cabs and big trucks fought loudly to move through the traffic laden streets. Everywhere I looked there was a flower shop. I could not wait to settle in so I could call upon all those prospects. Dallas was looking out the window for the nightclubs - that was okay, we needed them too. We got to Central Park and I could hardly contain my enthusiasm. Then the driver pulled up in front of one of the most extravagant buildings and stopped.

He said with a bit of a flourish, "Ladies, here you are." A doorman came out, got our bags and took us upstairs. We were on the top floor of one of the most beautiful buildings I had ever set foot in. A maid greeted us at the door. Inside, there were two bedrooms, two bathrooms and a beautiful living room that faced Central Park. We had the fanciest address in New York - 100 Central Park South. Thank you, Sammy.

Once we had seen our beautiful new digs, I couldn't wait to meet our benefactor Ronnie. I wondered if perhaps he lived in one of the bedrooms. I didn't know much about him, but since it was Sammy that hooked me up I knew he would not put me in a bad place.

After we put our things away, Dallas and I ran around our new neighborhood checking it out. We found a cool place to eat dinner and went to bed early so we could begin our new future first thing the following day.

I called Ronnie the next morning as I was eager to meet him. He told us to get in a cab and go to a deli on 49th. I had no idea what kind of a person I was looking for but when we walked in he knew exactly which ones we were. As usual, he immediately gravitated toward Dallas. She was such a man magnet.

Ronnie turned out to be a very large man. He must have weighed in the three hundred pound range, was in his mid-forties with thinning brown hair and light blue eyes. All during breakfast, Ronnie barely looked down at his hearty meal; those pale eyes were glued to Dallas. I really didn't care. I was grateful for his generosity and good taste in apartment buildings but couldn't imagine thanking him in the way he seemed to want. Let him lust after Dallas - I had work to do.

Like all New Yorkers Ronnie was in a hurry. He quickly planned our evening; we were to meet him at Studio 54 at ten o'clock - and off he went.

I needed to go back to the flower shop belonging to the guy with the warehouse and tried to persuade Dallas to go with me but she had no interest in work. Joey had sent her to the Big Apple with her pockets chock full of money to hold her over until he could come. She wanted to go spend some of her "hard earned" cash. So while she went shopping at Bergdorf's, I went shopping for warehouses. Louie, the warehouse owner, remembered me as I walked in. He asked if I wanted to see the warehouse right away so we got in his delivery van and off we went.

Louie and I pulled up in front of a broken down warehouse. I wondered if I had made a mistake but when we went inside it was perfect. There was a freezer, a greenhouse and lots of office space. It had been vacant for years and was cheap. My heart was racing with excitement. I told him I wanted it but could not pay him the rent until I got things going. He was great and agreed to let me pay him in flowers and greens until I had enough money.

When we got back to his store, I asked if I could call Julio. I'm sure he could feel my energy over the phone as I described how fortuitous it was that I met Louie on that wedding weekend. Julio was as thrilled as I was and told me to go for it. He said he would send me product right away, along with one of his trucks so I could make deliveries. We were not going to be partners. I just couldn't do that one again. I committed to buy exclusively from him and I would be his distributor in NY. The flowers and the truck arrived within two weeks. This time I was going to start small with me as the salesperson and one driver to make deliveries.

Later that evening, Dallas and I got all dressed up. I put on my tight black leather pants, high boots and a sexy silk top that showed just enough to provoke interest. Dallas wore a black mini skirt with high boots.

We looked amazing. We took a cab to the famous Studio 54. When we pulled up, there must have been a thousand people standing in line trying to get in. It felt like we were going to the Oscars. There were limos and actors and models and paparazzi snapping the more famous and outrageous ones. I saw lots of old rich men with beautiful young girls cuddling close to their patrons. We were meeting Ronnie there and I was hoping I was not going to look like all that arm candy. Dallas never cared whom her money came from or what she represented. Between her mother's twisted values and what she learned from Ike's other girls, Dallas knew exactly what she looked like. In her mind the benefits were well worth it.

With such a huge crowd I wasn't sure how we would get in. Within two minutes I got a tap on my shoulder from a large man who told me to follow him. He took us to a back entrance and led us right to the champagne room. There was big ole Ronnie with a doublewide grin.

Ronnie had a friend with him named Barry. Like Ronnie, he was an older gentleman but with distinguished looks. He was wearing a very expensive suit and a beautiful, Rolex, he had dark hair with a splash of gray. I always thought that look was sexy. Ronnie once again could not take his eyes of Dallas.

After two bottles of Dom Perignon, Barry was getting drunk. I loved my champagne but after being drugged that time by Charlie I always took it slow and did not let myself get out of control.

In conversation, I discovered they were both married, which of course didn't stop them. Barry was all over me; I could hardly control him. He was trying to rip my blouse off right there in the club. I was doing what I could to keep my composure and not make a scene while hanging on to my clothes. Then he moved onto bribery and offered me any amount of money or drugs I wanted.

I was insulted. I wanted to go back to being "the smart one."

Dallas had her hands full with Ronnie the giant, but she loved it; another rich, married man lusting after her, promising her the world. Now she could have one in New York and one in Miami.

As the evening moved on, Barry got way out of control. He was relentlessly lunging at me, slobbery drunk with hands that never stopped grabbing at me. He got so obnoxious I had to slap him. This angered him and he got in his Bentley and drove away. So much for getting *myself* a sugar daddy. I just couldn't go for it. About four in the morning, Ronnie dropped Dallas and me off at our (Ronnie's) magnificent apartment.

Dallas slept most of the day while I had about one hour of sleep before I had to get to my new flower warehouse. And so began the daily schedule: after a long morning of making hundreds of calls to retail flower shops, introducing myself as their new supplier, I would come home and take a nap. When I woke up a few hours later, Dallas would have plans for the evening all worked out.

Dallas' new affair with Ronnie was advantageous for both of us. He lavished her with the best of everything and made sure that she had all the designer clothes available and would treat us both to get our hair done by one of the top hairdresser's in New York. Both Ronnie and Dallas were good to me.

New York suited us. She was nineteen and I was twenty-one. We were introduced to some of the best places the city has to offer. We looked hot and dressed to kill. I'm glad Dallas and I were the same size because she was generous with all the expensive clothes Ronnie would bestow upon her. She was so damn beautiful that when we walked down the street traffic would stop and stare. With her similarity to Brooke Shields, everyone thought she was a supermodel. To say nothing of the many people who recognized her from Penthouse. They were still selling the magazine because she became Pet of the year.

Ronnie also saw her model qualities and set up an interview with the Ford Modeling Agency. I took her there and as we sat in the waiting room for about twenty minutes looking at thirty or so of the most beautiful and exotic women in the world, Dallas became aware of the competition. She grabbed my hand and pulled me the hell out of there.

One night we were out and stumbled on a male strip club called Chippendales. I loved the concept. Finally, women were outwardly gawking at beautiful men wearing next to nothing. The men were gyrating in their skimpy costumes with bare chests and six-pack abs. We found the champagne room and ordered a bottle. I always drank champagne even if I didn't have the money. My maxim was: you must think rich and you'll be rich. Luckily I didn't always have to buy, but I never let anyone think I couldn't have.

That night we met two of the cutest dancers. Will went for Dallas and Carl was into me. Now, this was fun! I was surprised, though, because Dallas never dated anyone who didn't have gobs of money at the ready to toss her way. All Will had to offer was the tips women stuffed into his tiny underwear - and his good looks and unbelievable body.

Carl was the same. I liked turning the tables and having him for arm candy. Dallas and I would wine and dine them and treat them very well. Dallas would use the money she got from both Ronnie and Joey and lavish it on her personal little Chippendale.

We became fixtures at the club. First, we would go out with Ronnie or Joey - whoever was Dallas' "Daddy of the Night" and we would finish off at Chippendales where the cute ones danced for us. Sometimes we would take them home. Dallas was a master at juggling daddies. She would weave elusive tales to Ronnie whenever Joey came up. It wasn't all that hard because he could never come for long. It was a quick lunch, shopping and a romp in the hotel room. She didn't dare take him to Ronnie's apartment, but she did charge Joey for her half of the rent that Ronnie wasn't charging. She rejected my suggestion that she be open with all her benefactors. After all, they were both married to someone else. But Dallas thought it was better to secretly keep them both and have a few poor Chippies on the side.

Dallas had a big heart and would help anyone. I think that's one of the reasons we got along so well as I was the same way. The only difference is that I had to work hard for my money. I always said that if someone needed it more than me (and that was hard because I was pretty broke and far from having my millions) I would give him or her what I could.

Life in New York was wild and fun for both of us. However, Dallas started getting a little out of control. Her drug addiction was growing stronger and she became sloppy about being with different male partners every night. It started to bother me. I would come home from having worked from six in the morning to six at night, the apartment would be a wreck and she would just be getting up. She was spending money like it was nothing on cocaine and her young men. When I would ask for half of the Florida townhouse rent she no longer had it.

Ronnie started doing business in Atlantic City. He would have a helicopter pick us up in Manhattan on a Saturday night and have us back home by Sunday night. I didn't know what he did for a living but I knew better than to ask. We would hang out in the casino and watch Ronnie play baccarat for a thousand dollars per hand. It was quite exciting. Especially the times when he would win over one hundred thousand dollars - and sometimes he would lose that much. Either way, he was always generous and fun.

My flower business was booming. Getting some of my vendors to pay me was difficult. Most of my clients were not in the nicest neighborhoods in the Bronx, Brooklyn and Harlem. That's when I wished I had someone like Jeff around. I asked Carl if he didn't mind showing off those beautiful muscles to help me with collections. He thought it would be fun; I still had my 25 automatic. Within three days, we had all the money. After that business was good.

I flew back and forth once a month to see Julio, check on the quality of the product and make sure all was well with my townhouse. For some reason, Avi would always know when I was home. I had been in New York for quite some time and had finally come to my senses about our relationship. Although I held a special place in my heart for him, I finally had the will to resist him.

I pushed my deadline to be a millionaire back one more year. I was doing quite well, but not in the millions. One day I was sitting in my office answering phones and Trudy called. At first I thought she was going to tell me that Avi had broken up with his wife because she found out about us. What Trudy had to say was so much more startling.

She started by telling me to sit down. When someone starts off with those words you imagine the most terrible things, but I could *never* have guessed what it turned out to be. She told me I was on the front page of the Miami Herald and was being indicted for twenty-one counts of fraud and conspiracy. It named me as the owner of the oil company that Billy owned. What? I didn't own that company! It had to be a mistake. She went on to report that Billy had turned witness and had given me up as the mastermind. That was impossible. I was only twenty when I subleased the place to that sleaze. I thanked Trudy for the information and sat there in shock.

Chapter 15
THE TWO SAMMYS

Trudy had faxed me a copy of the paper. It said, "If anyone has information as to the whereabouts of Gigi Kapchuk-Nassar contact the Postal Inspectors Office immediately." My heart was racing. I did not know what Billy could have said to get me into this much trouble and couldn't see a way out. I contacted the Postal Inspectors Office at the Federal building in Miami. They warned me I had twenty-four hours to turn myself in. I told them I was living in NYC and argued that didn't do anything wrong. They didn't much care. They repeated, "Just report to Brooklyn County Jail no later than two p.m. tomorrow."

I didn't know what to do or who to call. My primal instinct was to call my Mom but the reality was I couldn't trust her to be my champion. We had been through several bouts of not speaking to each other and this was one of them. I tried to call Dallas who was useless; she was sleeping off another wild drug night and did not answer the phone. I then called someone reliable with clout - Sammy. He made some calls and then told me to get in a cab and go straight to the Brooklyn jail right then. Horrified and scared, and with *no* lawyer, I got in a cab and did what he told me.

Reluctantly, I instructed the cab driver to take me to the jail in Brooklyn. He asked me if I was visiting someone. I let him believe that because I didn't want him to think of me as a criminal - especially because I was *not*. I was shaking. I had no idea what would happen to me. What if they locked me up and no one knew I was there? How would I ever get out?

I slowly walked up the driveway ready to change my mind.

They don't know where I am. I don't own anything. How would they find me? Maybe I can make it go away.

But I was way too terrified to run. My only hope was Sammy, but that was growing smaller since it was he was the one who told me to go to jail! I walked in the main door and asked which department a person should go to if they were turning themselves in. The man on the phone pointed me toward a police officer who directed me to go to the jail. So, I walked myself over to the jail. Was I dreaming? I wished.

The hallway was filled with criminals handcuffed to benches, cops yelling, victims crying. Where did I fit in? I walked up to the scary officer at the counter and gave him my name. He typed it into the computer and a few minutes later, in a tone usually associated with a maître d, he said, "Gigi, oh yes. We were expecting you. Come this way." He read me my rights which I didn't really understand because he said them so fast. Then he took me into a smaller room where a lady cop was waiting for me. She told me to take off all my clothes so she could examine me. It took me forever. What could she have been looking for? Fake oil contracts? After I got down to my bra and panties (pretty ones from Ronnie, indirectly) she gave me a look like I had not completed the task so I asked, "More?"

She lifted one bushy eyebrow and said callously, "All."

I was disgusted. She then rubbed her cold hands up and down my thin body. It was so intimidating and humiliating. What the hell could she be looking for? After that she told me to put on orange pants and shirt with a number on it. From that point on, I was no longer Gigi. I was handed a wooden board with a number that matched my clothes. I was to hold it while they took photographs of me - front view and both sides. I had come a long way from the modeling photos I almost did.

After the "photo shoot," they put me in a holding cell with six other women. It smelled like urine and throw up. Most of the women were prostitutes - some were drug dealers. All I could think was "What the hell am I doing here?"

No one came in or said a word to me. The other girls, most of whom had been there before, told me to just go to sleep and someone would be there by morning.

"Morning?" I yelled. "I have to sleep here?"

They laughed. A Puerto Rican woman with a broken tooth said, "Sit down, Princess."

I looked around. There were only two benches, which were taken up already. There was only one toilet in the corner with no curtain. There was no way I was going to go to the bathroom there. After about four hours of pacing and hoping for a rescue, I gave up. I sat down on the filthy floor, put my arms tight around my legs, dropped my chin to my knees and waited. I was tired but was so keyed up I couldn't sleep. In any case, the cacophony of people walking back and forth, keys jangling, and doors to the interrogation room next to us opening and closing and all the angry people loudly protesting their arrests, would have kept even the drugged ones awake. It was the longest night of my life.

Finally, at eight in the morning, an officer came in to take me before the judge. They put handcuffs on me and walked me to the courtroom. I looked at the officer as if to say - I weigh all of one hundred pounds; I'm charged with tricking people into buying bogus oil property in Alaska, which I didn't do, by the way... do you really think you need those cuffs? He ignored my look.

So there I was, pathetically standing in front of a judge with no lawyer. He read some papers and looked down at me. He said flatly, "Young lady, you are free to go from here. You have been extradited to Florida, which means you have twenty-four hours to get there and get council. You are hereby released on your own recognizance until your arraignment in Florida."

The officer removed the cuffs and took me to the property room to get my belongings and change into my clothes. I was out of there as soon as possible.

I have never been late to work. It was eleven in the morning before I got to the shop. Everyone was worried. I was relieved to see that the new sales girl I had hired and the driver had done a good job keeping it together with both sales and deliveries. We finished the day like nothing happened. I didn't want to upset the applecart, if you know what I mean.

I called Sammy and reported the latest. He assured me he had a good criminal lawyer in Florida – one who represented all the big drug dealers.

The lawyer had the exact name as my Sammy. That's how they met. They would keep getting each other's calls and eventually became close friends. My Sammy did a three-way call with Sammy, the lawyer. They both advised me to be on the first flight in the morning and meet the lawyer at the Federal Building at eleven a.m. The last thing he said was, "Bring your checkbook and I'll see you tomorrow."

I got some of the important bills in order, organized schedules and told the employees I had to go to Florida to see Julio. This was not unusual since I did that all the time. I signed their payroll checks just in case I didn't make it back by that Friday.

I went home to see if Dallas even knew I had been missing for the night. When I walked in, she was just getting home herself. She had invited another girl to stay with us. Her name was Patty and she was dating Barry, the friend of Ronnie's I had slapped that first night in New York. They were all still a little high and crazy. I decided not to discuss my night. I simply told them I had to go to Florida and would be back in a few days.

I had just gone through twenty-four hours of jail and judges without any sleep so I went straight to bed. I needed to be fresh to deal with my new, complicated life. It was hard to drift off to sleep knowing that I was unfairly arrested - all because of that sleaze ball Billy.

I took the seven a.m. flight to Miami, grabbed a cab and went to the Federal Building desperately looking for my new lawyer. The building was very intimidating. It was tall with lots of security. I took the elevator to the tenth floor. Each floor seemed to go by in slow motion and all I could think about was going back to a disgusting jail. I could not endure another night there. I knew I was not guilty of anything except being stupid enough to befriend Billy. What I could not predict was whether or not there were any laws that would protect me from such a lying scoundrel?

I got out of the elevator and walked to the hallway in front of the courtroom and was met by a young, handsome man who asked if I was Gigi. I replied with a very timid voice, "Yes, that's me." He introduced himself as Sammy, my lawyer, even though I had not hired him yet and was not at all sure if I could afford him. I was told he was very expensive.

He was not what I had expected and though I was a little enamored with his "kind of young - kind of cute" looks, when he spoke it was a different story. He said he had been reading up on the case and explained that Billy had made a deal and told authorities that I was the owner along with two of his partners. One of the partners had pled guilty and was facing thirty years in prison. All the employees were being indicted too. Sammy told me that this case was very serious and that I was facing the distinct possibility of going to prison.

"We are about to go before the judge to be arraigned," he said with authority. "I'll try to convince the judge to let you out on bail while I prepare your case."

I felt numb. It was hard to collect my thoughts.

Sammy asked, "Do you have any evidence regarding the oil deals that were sold?"

"No. I was only the landlord. I tried to sell the product but I didn't believe in it, so I never made any sales. I was not an owner or partner with that crook."

As I stood before the judge, I felt like a trapped animal. What if he didn't let me out on bail? What if he made the bail so high I couldn't pay?

When Sammy spoke to the judge he was cool and relaxed as if he didn't have a concern in the world. He was so carefree I thought maybe he was just an actor. Or maybe he simply did not care what happened to me.

Sammy asked the judge to release me to him while he prepared my case. The judge looked at me with one eye and asked, "Young lady, do you understand the seriousness of this case?"

I said, "Yes sir" with all the respect and good manners I could conjure up even though I didn't actually know how bad it really was. How could they charge me when I didn't do anything but keep my mouth shut?

The judge granted our wish, but he told me I had to be booked and then I could be released. The deputy took me away. Sammy told me he would wait for me outside the jail to make sure I got released. The officer took me to a booking room that looked so familiar I started to shake again. How could I be sure I wouldn't have to spend the night again? I hung on to the fact that Sammy promised I would get out right away. Inside it was a little nicer because everyone there had been charged with a federal crime. On the bright side, I guess they were upscale criminals.

This time they had me put on brown clothes but did not do a body search. I got my mug shot taken again and within an hour I was released. Sammy gave me a ride to my townhouse, and we made an appointment for the next morning to go over fees and sign paperwork.

Friend Sammy came over to take me out to dinner so I could fill him in on the details. The two Sammys at this point were the only ones that knew - thankfully none of my friends read the paper.

Morning came early and I dressed in one of my sexiest outfits to meet my new handsome lawyer. When I walked into his office I could see right away that he had done his homework. He knew everything about me; the construction company, my father, my tenth grade education, the race track - everything. He asked me for $75,000. I almost choked. I told him the most I could do right then was $10k - and that was taking everything I had. He was nice and agreed to take that as a deposit. I gave him the check and signed a contract.

He then asked me if I could meet him later because he had to go to court and couldn't finish our meeting. We agreed to meet at the Forge, the elite restaurant I used to go with Robert and Joey. I showed up at eight wearing one of my most alluring Cavalli dresses.

I couldn't keep my eyes off him. He was so powerful and was in charge of my future; I found that to be very appealing. We talked about my case for only about five minutes - mostly because I didn't have much to say. I didn't know anything. The rest of the time we drank my favorite bottle of Chateau Laffite then we washed that down with a bottle of Chateau de Caim. We were both a little tipsy - well, he was drunk. We stayed until almost closing, talking about his impending divorce. I was happy to hear that.

He paid the very large check and we left. He lived around the corner so he asked if I could drive him. I was more than happy to accommodate. We got in my car and before I could put on my seatbelt, he reached over and gave me the most amazing kiss. I thought I was powerless before, but now I was hopeless. Here I was, meeting my lawyer to help me repudiate some serious charges against me and yet, in his arms, I forgot about my sobering problems. Well, tomorrow was another day. We kissed in the car for hours like teenagers at a drive-in movie. By dawn we had to face reality - he had a busy day and I had to figure out how I was going to pay him the rest of his fees. So we said good night and I drove off.

That afternoon I went to visit Julio. It was only fair to tell him what happened. I was worried about his reaction. What if he thought I was a criminal? What if he didn't want to supply flowers to me anymore? How would I pay Sammy? Ahhh, is there ever an easy day? To my surprise, Julio understood. I convinced him I hadn't done anything and he believed me as I had never lied to him before. He promised to keep supplying me as long as my indictment didn't interfere with my work.

After Julio's reaction I decided to tell Avi. I was beginning to trust that my true friends would believe me and not be so judgmental. It was always difficult to see Avi, but I needed his friendship. I had so much on my mind and I wanted to talk it out with someone who not only knew me; he cared about me. He wasn't around.

The next possible person to go to for support was my mother. Call me crazy, but I went to her house. She already knew. One of her friends had seen it in the paper. I was surprised and a little hurt that Mom didn't call me to see how I was, since she had known for about a week. She didn't have any motherly advice for me; she just needed to tell me that I shouldn't have done it. I hoped she meant that I shouldn't have trusted that man to sublease from me, but I doubted she understood.

I went back to New York the next day to keep the flower company going. Dallas and Patty were home waiting for me. I had given Dallas the short version over the phone and she was very upset. She told Ronnie and

Joey and they were all genuinely concerned. Playtime was the usual way of handling things in their world, so the girls thought I needed a night out. Ronnie arranged a party at Club A - the newest, hottest club in the city. We drank champagne and ate caviar till three a.m. I was feeling a little guilty partying like I didn't have a care in the world. Ronnie was spending money like water and all I could think was, "I could be spending that on my lawyer so I don't have go to jail."

The next morning, I went to the warehouse at six a.m. to get a jumpstart on sales. I knew I had to double the business to pay the bills and the lawyer. I started calling on new clients. I got the phone book for all the counties in the area and starting getting new accounts.

Joey called me from Florida to see how I was. Joey had originally started out as my friend from the racetrack. I was the one who introduced him to Dallas, and we ended up being closer. Things were changing with Dallas. The drugs had taken over. Her addiction was running her life at that point and there was barely any room for either Joey or Ronnie. They both knew it. It wouldn't be long before both her sugar daddies would give up on her. I was worried about the rent money. Joey had been paying Dallas' half of my place both in Florida and the city. I needed that cushion. Every dime I had was going to my lawyer.

In the course of our conversation, Joey told me he had a new girlfriend. Her name was Laura. Joey wanted to set up the same arrangement as he had with Dallas. Of course I agreed - I was always the responsible one taking care of everyone. I discussed it with Ronnie because even though Laura was in Florida, she would also be coming to New York regularly. He thought it was just fine, but needed me to move out. Having us live in the apartment had been helping him with rent control, but the building was going co-op.

Ronnie had another place for me, so I moved to the West Side to a beautiful building overlooking the other side of Central Park. It was amazing. Ronnie said I could only stay there for a few months. I didn't mind. I was excited anyway.

Dallas moved with me. She had been getting on my nerves. She would go on binges for days. Her sloppy dating with men coming and going made me very uncomfortable, as well. Just about everyone was getting tired of Dallas the Drug Addict.

My flower business was picking up. Thanks to my long hours and persistence, we were getting a lot of new accounts. I was driven by fear.

I had to go back to Florida to see my lawyer and meet my new roommate, Laura. Thanks to Joey, she had already moved into my townhouse. Laura was pretty - not Dallas pretty - but pretty enough. She had short blonde hair, blue eyes and, although she was thin, she was no hot Penthouse Pet.

After meeting Laura, I went straight to see Sammy the lawyer to discuss my case. The very first thing he said was he needed more money. He told me to give him five thousand dollars more right away. I was not prepared, but I gave him the money that was supposed to go back into the business. Sammy didn't have anything else to tell me other than he was working on evidence. So, I flirted a little and he said he would call me later and I left.

Joey came over and took Laura and me to dinner at The Palm. We had a lovely time. It reminded me of the old days. I was living like nothing particular was different, except that all my money was going to Sammy the lawyer.

I stayed in Florida for a few more days acquiring new growers, showing new flowers and finding more products to sell in New York. I spent my nights with

Laura and Joey. He was so cool. We would go to Joe's Stone Crabs - an impossible place to get into without waiting at least an hour - but we would walk right in and sit down.

I flew back to the city with my new product ideas - minus five thousand dollars. It was back to working twelve-hour days.

Dallas was doing her usual. She looked awful - like the walking dead. It was a shame. That once beautiful girl had thrown it all away for coke. I tried to get her help but she wouldn't listen. It was very depressing to watch her go down like that. She and Patty would get stoned all day. Patty would use Barry and then cheat on him, sometimes three times in one night. She was disgusting. One night she was stoned and took off all her clothes and made a move on my Chippendale, Carl. I was so furious I told Barry what a slut she was. I guess they had a fight after that because I woke up with Patty on top of me beating me with a shoe. She finally packed her stuff and left.

Two weeks passed when my lawyer's office called and told me I needed to be back in Florida for a preliminary hearing the following week.

The second I stepped foot in Sammy's office he asked me for another five grand. I reluctantly gave him the money I was supposed to give Julio for supplies. He didn't care. He told me that I had a choice: either go to jail or give him more money to work hard. We prepared for the hearing that was taking place the next day.

Back in front of the judge, I was once again at the mercy of others and could not believe I was fighting for my life when there were rapists and murderers out there.

Sammy talked to the judge and presented the evidence. He sounded so sexy when he talked. He was so powerful. They were speaking their special legalese and the next thing I knew the hearing was over. I didn't really know what had happened. It seemed like an easy decision. After all, it was clearly not my fault.

But it was far from over.

Chapter 16
JUDGMENT DAY

I went home disgusted. Had I scraped up all that money just so Sammy could have a little "chat" with the judge? We were no closer to a decision. Even though I was stressed about the impending result, I was still foolishly enamored with my handsome lawyer. Later that night he called saying he wanted to come over. I couldn't wait.

Laura was at the apartment. I was hoping she would go out, but she didn't get the hint.

When he arrived, I melted. He was just so damn cute. Laura immediately moved in on him. She sat next to him and started flirting. He was eating it up. After only about twenty minutes of it, I became highly irritated with both of them. The next thing I knew she came out with this big bag of coke and they started getting high together. It went on all night. They were talking shit that didn't make sense. I could not believe my lawyer was a cokehead. I locked myself in my room and went to bed. He was gone by morning.

I flew back to NY to make more money to supply his habit. A week later his office called and told me Sammy was coming to the city and wanted to meet with me. They said he had some important things to discuss.

It was the Christmas season in New York. Snow sat on windowsills and people were bustling trying to get the perfect gifts. It felt romantic in the city and I had the notion that Sammy would feel the same. Within five minutes of his arrival, he asked me for cocaine. I suppose if I had been a little older and more confident I would have kicked him to the curb, but I felt stuck with a drug addict for a lawyer and was afraid to make him angry. He constantly threatened that if it weren't for him I'd be in jail. I knew Joey had kept some drugs in the spare room so I gave him some. He got high and I watched. I finally went to bed and he let himself out.

All this pressure was killing me. Two weeks went by and I got another call from Sammy's office demanding another payment of five grand. I told his assistant that I didn't have it. I couldn't take anymore. I still hadn't paid Julio for the products yet. Sammy's demands were becoming too much. His assistant curtly announced that he would call me the next day.

When he called, he said if I didn't pay him he would resign from my case and I would go to jail. Stressed, broke and disillusioned, I went to Ronnie and borrowed the five thousand.

I told Sammy I had the money. He told me to bring it to him and he would make arrangements to see the judge again.

When I arrived in Florida, I went straight to his office. He was leaning back against his desk with an air of entitlement.

"You brought the five?"

I gave it to him as usual.

"Look, Gigi, if you can't get your hands on another twenty thousand, you should just plead guilty. This case is just too expensive. Don't worry about it. The fact that you're so young and they have no evidence, you'll probably just get some probation. It's no big deal."

There was no way I could dig up twenty thousand. I was scared out of my mind and felt I had no choice but to trust him. I reminded myself over and over that I didn't do anything wrong, so everything should be fine.

The next day I was standing before the judge again, but this time I had Sammy beside me. The judge asked me if I was changing my plea. Sammy told me to answer YES. I hesitated. Sammy said it was better to agree and say yes so the judge would see I was cooperating.

Coupled with the fact that I was only twenty-one and had no prior arrests, Sammy assured me that the judge was sure to go easy on me. And I wouldn't owe him any more money. I reluctantly changed my plea to guilty.

The judge took a minute before he said anything. The disapproving look on his face forced me to look away in shame. I stared down at my old designer shoes and started shaking again knowing I had just put my life in the hands of a crooked cokehead.

It was a relief when the judge finally broke the silence. "Ms. Nassar, did you know what you were doing to those people when you stole their money?"

I was about to say I didn't do anything, but Sammy answered before I could open my mouth. "Yes, your Honor, she knew what she was doing, but she's *very* sorry."

The judge slammed his hammer down, gave both of us a dirty look and said, "Come back in two weeks for sentencing. Court adjourned."

I didn't move right away. I was in shock. That was it? I just told a judge that I was guilty of something I did not do and that I was sorry for hurting people I never called? Sammy assured me that this was just a formality and not to worry. Easy for him to say; he was going back to his office to get high.

I flew back to NY to pack my things in case I got probation. This seemed likely and meant that I would not be able to travel as much. I pleaded with both Julio and my employees to keep working to help me keep everything I had worked for. I promised them that as soon as this was over I would be back and would reward them for their efforts.

Within a week, I was back in Florida waiting my turn to see the judge who had my future in his hands. I hung out with Laura, Joey and friends of his at The Palm.

Finally, the day came. I was thinking it was going to be a huge relief because Sammy kept assuring me, "After all, they don't throw twenty-two-year-old girls with no priors in jail."

I walked into the courtroom with Sammy, impatient to get it over with. There were so many people in the room and I didn't know who they all were. What if they were the victims of the oil scam? My lawyer and I sat in the middle. The clock on the wall behind me sounded like the old ones from school where you could hear the minute hand click to the next peg. It seemed like hours between each click.

Sammy whispered that the other people were some of the other employees and their representatives. I was feeling more and unsure of my lawyer and my circumstances as I looked around the small room.

We had thirty minutes of torturous silence before the judge arrived. He came in with a purposeful walk. The bailiff said, "All rise." He sounded so serious. I could hardly stand it, but was truly grateful for Sammy's continuous reassurance that everything would be just fine.

After a long introduction of all members of the court by the judge, he then called me to the stand. Both Sammy and I approached the bench. The judge began reciting the statutes of the case and then asked me if I understood that I was changing my plea from not guilty to guilty. My instinct was screaming at me to tell the truth. I did not want to say it, but I whispered, "Yes." I was so quiet he had to ask me again. I repeated, "Yes, your Honor." Everything in my being told me to say, "Stop. Wait. I need you to know what really happened. I cannot admit to something I didn't do!" But I just stood there quietly like a bad little girl.

His Honor looked at me with disdain, like a father would after he caught his daughter having sex in her parents' room with a greasy boyfriend. I closed my eyes. I wanted this whole thing to go away. Knowing now full well what was coming next, I started praying.

"Ms. Nassar. You have done a terrible thing. You have hurt innocent people with your malicious greed. I hereby sentence you to SIX MONTHS in Dade County Corrections Jail, FIVE YEARS probation, FIVE HUNDRED HOURS of community service, and a FIVE THOUSAND dollar fine."

My eyes widened. I looked at my useless lawyer who seemed to be even more surprised than I was. At that point I think if Sammy asked me for one more penny, I would have gone to jail for murder instead.

"You must report to the Women's Detention Center in Miami within ninety days from today to start your sentence. You are NOT to leave town and you must stay away from telephone sales."

Well, that didn't go well.

So, after bleeding my company and walking away with nothing, as I couldn't even go back to New York, I wondered if in the end I really needed the cute cokehead lawyer for anything other than bail and eye candy. Could I have done a worse job by myself?

I called Julio to give him the news. I made a deal with him that he could keep everything I had at the warehouse. Most of all, I felt bad about all my sales girls and driver. They depended on me for their jobs.

So now, with no job, no money and soon no freedom, I was about to turn twenty-two... and still no millions.

Red Mare

We Loved LuLu

Ivan and Me

Early Beginnings

Dancing Queen

Miami Beach Cheesecake Model

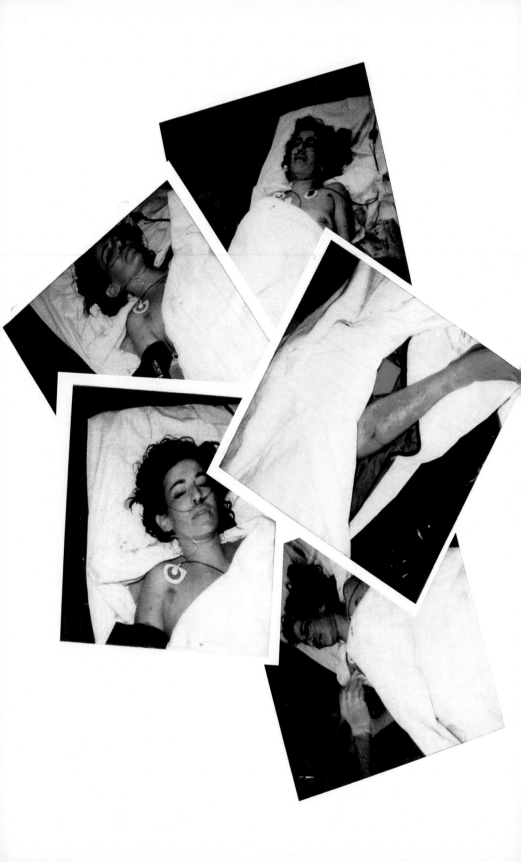

Bring it On

Lost Dance Contest to Mom

Turnberry, Here I Come

Chapter 17
CO-RECEIVER

Lulu once told me that when one door closes another one opens. That became my mantra and helped me through every disaster or disappointment that had threatened my happiness.

I called my real friend Sammy and told him what happened. He was shocked and felt bad that he had recommended the other Sammy. We talked about filing an appeal but that sounded too expensive. In the meantime, he needed me. His hotels were doing badly. He was in a financial mess and asked if I would work for him running the five hotels and help to get them sold.

It sounded challenging. He told me he couldn't pay me much but he really needed me. I didn't have anything else to do for the three months prior to going to my new living quarters. I would have helped him no matter what.

I decided to tell my mother what had happened. She was still dating a man name Jerry. He was sort of cool and very smart. He never had children. My mother had been dating him on and off since I was sixteen, but I didn't really know him then. He had a fatherly quality about him and I liked him enough. I used to joke around with him and call him daddy. I didn't see what his interest was in my mother, but I didn't really care. When Mom told Jerry what had happened to me he wanted to see me right away. He thought he could help. I met them at his place at the Jockey Club. We had dinner at the club and talked about the case. He asked the names of the judge and lawyer, as if he knew everyone. I figured he was someone because he had a limo, a Bentley and a Mercedes in the driveway.

I filled my belly with gourmet cuisine since I was not sure how my future looked in the food department. I talked to him about Sammy and the hotels. I had only been there for two days but I was ready to take over. Sammy was really having a hard time. He was a little depressed because he was losing everything and was about to file bankruptcy. Jerry was very interested in the project.

My first week on the job I faced creditors and Code Enforcement officers leaving fines at the door and threatening to condemn the building. One of his buildings was an ACLF (Adult Congregate Living Facility) that served kosher meals to the old Jewish retirees who lived there. It was such a sad situation and I was determined to set things right before I "went away".

Sammy could not afford a lawyer to help him with the code violations, so I took that job. I figured with the amount of time I spent in court and with lawyers, I could give it a try.

When I arrived at the hotel, Sammy told me we had a final hearing on fifteen violations. If we lost they would close the ACLF hotel - which was his main source of income. With my experience in the construction business, I took a look at the violations. Some I got repaired right away and tried to get an extension for the rest.

Two weeks later it was time for the hearing. I couldn't believe I was going back to court again. The whole job was so interesting - juggling creditors, trying to salvage money, giving a little to everyone so they would keep supplying.

This courthouse was nothing like I was use to. It was just an old one-story building.

The room was full of firemen and inspectors. The judge called the defendant to the bench. I guessed that meant me since I was representing Sammy, the hotel owner. I was his manager.

By the time I was done presenting my evidence, offering to make certain repairs within forty-eight hours and arguing that some did not exist, the judge told me to make two repairs and everything else was dismissed.

Almost every night I would have dinner with Jerry. Sometimes my mother would come, but most of the time she was out dancing and doing occasional photography work. Jerry was fascinating to me: he was trying to figure out how to capitalize on Sammy's misfortune. Being loyal to Sammy, I was determined to work it so they both could benefit. I suggested that Jerry give a bridge loan to Sammy to relieve some of his stress - and it would make Jerry a very good return. They both agreed. It wasn't long before I brought Jerry a pile of money for the large amount he made from the loan fees. Meanwhile, Sammy got some credit relief until we could get something sold.

Jerry began mentoring me. It was all so exciting. He let me sit in on huge deals. Sometimes he would negotiate as much as twenty million dollars, buying companies that were in trouble. Other times he'd buy one for next to nothing then fix it and resell it. I was in heaven. It was all so stimulating. Too bad I only had a couple of months left.

At night Sammy and I were back as the party team. I would forget about doomsday and Sammy would let go of foreclosures. We had a routine where we would visit different clubs every night. He had plenty of girlfriends. I found him very attractive, but we were more like siblings. We knew each other's secrets. It made our bond even stronger.

While wheeling and dealing with creditors and investors trying to fight foreclosures, Jerry would give me advice and we would strategize together to help Sammy hang on to his properties. I had a deal pending and we needed to keep the properties long enough for the buyers to close. On Jerry's recommendation, Sammy filed bankruptcy for protection. He hired a bankruptcy lawyer named John. I don't know if it was the fact that I was carrying around a bad taste in my mouth for lawyers in general, but he didn't seem that smart. But what did I know? I was just a twenty-two-year-old on her way to jail.

On top of the bankruptcy problems, we still had code violations piling up, though I felt like I had a handle on that. I was going back and forth to court for Sammy at least once a week about something or other. John, the bankruptcy lawyer, brought in his intern Barry to handle the code violations. Barry didn't have a clue. He was fresh out of school with a great diploma but couldn't find his way to the courtroom. I continued to handle the cases and Barry got all the credit and the pay. Oh well, I was used to that. The most important thing was to protect my dear friend.

The day finally came when I received a letter telling me where to go, what to do, who my probation officer was and to report to him within three days.

Party over.

I didn't know what to expect when I arrived at the office of Dan the Probation Man. He was a tall, thin, unshaven man who smelled like coffee and cigarettes. It was the same stench that Charlie had and it gave me the creeps. He barely said hello. I guess I was just another criminal to him.

He handed me a cup and told me to give him a urine sample. I had no idea why, but I went into the small bathroom and did it. When I gave the cup to him he said, "Get used to it. You will be drug tested once a week. I'll be doing' it randomly so don't get any ideas."

"Actually, that's not a problem. I'm not a drug addict. I'm here for fraud charges," I said in the sweetest tone I could scrape up. I doubted he even read my case.

I saw a pamphlet on his desk that said if I had a legitimate job I could actually work during the day and sleep at the facility at night. That would be great! Sammy needed me and Jerry and he were giving me an amazing business education. At the rate I was learning, going to jail would set me back five years.

I explained it all to Dan. He narrowed his eyes and said, "First, we must see if your urine is clean."

I knew that was not going to be a problem, so I started begging. I told him I would be his model prisoner. I thought I would leave the part out that the hotels were in bankruptcy and I was controlling all the money. He might not have liked that part.

I went to see him the following week and it was the same routine - urine test and more interrogation about my life. He asked me stuff that was not even related to me, but I killed him with kindness. He then told me my urine from last week had been clean, so he would let me try the work release program on a week-to-week basis. The rules were fairly simple; the only time I was allowed to be out was solely for my job, I needed to show Dan a time card, my supervisor must be fully aware of my circumstances and he needed to sign me in and out of the job. I knew Sammy would be thrilled, since I had pretty much taken over the day-to-day operations of his business. He would have been lost without me.

The night before my loss of freedom, Sammy and Jerry and I had a nice dinner at the Jockey Club. After that, I went to Turnberry with Laura and Joey. I partied all night without a single drink. Dan scared me so much I was even afraid to drink coffee.

The next morning I had a Code Enforcement hearing. I thought I would do that and then report in early to make a good impression. I didn't need to be there until five p.m. I won the hearing, got the hotel organized for the night shift and then drove myself to the Women's Detention Center.

Ever since I found out I had to go to the center, I pictured myself living in a cement building surrounded by barbed wire with armed guards pacing back and forth. I figured there must be some holding room where I would change into my orange jumpsuit and be sent off to some kind of small cell.

Pulling up to the facility, I was surprised to see what looked like an old hotel. There were gates in the front and the back that were only manned by one guard standing at a booth. I went up to the guard in the back where I parked my car, gave him my name and he let me in. He told me to go to the counter and register.

Since it was originally a hotel, there was a lobby that was used for recreation. It had a dining room and a few other small rooms that were used for interviews. That's where the girl at the counter told me to wait. Inside the tiny, dingy room were two chairs, a table and a dimly lit lamp. I waited, holding my small bag of clothes and toiletries, not knowing whether or not I should sit down when the door opened abruptly. A very large person - I was not sure whether it was man or women - walked in. Once she spoke, I was relieved of my speculation. The first thing she did was recite the rules in a way that sounded as if I had already broken them. I could tell she hated me. Then she demanded that I take all my clothes off.

As she struggled to get a rubber glove on her large hand, she commanded, "Bend over."

I was horrified. "What are you going to do?"

"What do you think?"

"I don't know," I responded.

She shoved me a little and repeated, "I said, bend over! Spread your legs and shut up."

How do you argue with that?

I felt raped.

"Why did you have to do that? I'm not here for drugs or weapons."

"Shut the fuck up." She then gave me a cup for a urine sample.

I was shaking. This brute of a woman would not even let me put on my clothes first. I begged her. She walked me over to a small toilet with one curtain and stood there. She wasn't going anywhere.

"Please, I don't think I can do this with you standing there. Can I please have some privacy?"

"NO. Hurry up. I don't have all night."

The stress of it took over and I could not release. I sat there for one hour, buck naked, shivering and still nothing came. Water was coming out of my eyes, but nowhere else. I was horrified. I didn't know what was wrong with me. I asked for a drink of water. Nothing. The monster woman was not about to budge. She thought I was hiding something. After one hour and fifty-five minutes, she told me she would have to draw blood. I was fine with that as long as I could do it with clothes on.

My initiation was over and then it was time to see my living quarters and meet my cellmate.

She walked me down a long corridor to the fifth door on the right. I started to sweat at the idea of being locked up. I wasn't sure I could go through with this. My heart was racing. I felt trapped and I hadn't even put one foot into the room yet. Monster Woman opened the door with her many keys and I hesitated. She would have none of it and grabbed my arm to "escort" me into a tiny room with two cots and a toilet with no door. There was also a small shower and one large window that had bars on. There was a small cot. I slept on the floor for months when Mother left my dad. Jail, it seemed, was a step up.

"Your bed WILL be made before you go to work," Monster bellowed. "The floor and room MUST be spotless. There will be inspections twice a day. All lights will be out by eight o'clock. You can go to the rec room until six p.m. There will be three meals served a day at seven a.m., twelve p.m. and five p.m." With that, she turned on her heels and left.

I had no intentions of eating that food. I would eat at the hotel before I came back.

My new cellmate sat expressionless on the cot watching my ordeal. Her name was Lucy. She was Spanish and spoke with a heavy accent. She welcomed me and immediately showed me the ropes. She told me who was who and how to get drugs inside and how to escape. That really wasn't the stuff I wanted to know but I listened anyway.

The monster left the door open because lockdown didn't happen until eight. I thought I would check things out and see what other kinds of people were staying at this "hotel". I walked toward the back and noticed that there was a men's side to the building. I thought that could brighten things up. Unfortunately there was a large fence between us. There were about thirty or so dirty looking, unshaven men all sitting around not looking too ambitious. On the women's side most were Latino or black. They were in there for drugs, dealing and prostitution. There was no one in for fake oil leases.

When it was almost six PM, I headed back to my hole. I saw Lucy in the hallway. She was headed there, too. We went inside and started chatting. She told me she had been there for three months and had six to go. She had been there before; it was her second offense. I asked why. She said drugs and asked me if I had any. I shook my head and asked how would I get them in? She then sat on the toilet, dropped her panties, spread her legs and pulled a bag of cocaine out of her vagina. I was stunned. Then she asked if I wanted some. I said I wasn't interested. All I could think of was *this girl is TROUBLE.* I just wanted to work and move on with my life. She was surprised I turned her down. Lucy then asked me if she could use my urine for the drug test. *So that's why Monster Woman did those things to me.* How did Lucy get away with it? Thank god it was lights out. I didn't really want a social life with another drug addict.

Seven a.m. couldn't come quick enough. I made my bed, tidied my area and took off to my hotel job. Things were hectic as usual. No money for bills and many more code violations. Just as I would clean up one pile of violations, inspectors came and gave me a new pile. I think they really didn't like Sammy. It was impossible to have that many. Even though we had that much trouble I loved it.

Unfortunately, I didn't get to have any more fancy dinners with Jerry, but I would talk to him every day. He wanted to know everything that was going on since his money was in one of the hotels and he held the mortgage.

With so much to do, the end of the day would come way too soon. I had to grab a bite to eat and then head out to my hole before five.

As I pulled into the parking lot, I noticed a very cute guy parking next to me. He was noticing me too. I thought that might be too complicated, so I locked my car door and went inside. Monster Woman was standing there holding a cup again. I wondered if I had to do this every night how *did* Lucy do it. Monster followed me into the bathroom again. This time it only took forty-five minutes to pee. I got another speech from the monster and then went to my hole.

Lucy was not there yet. She had ten minutes to be inside. I didn't really like her, but I was concerned for her. I didn't want her to get in trouble. She finally showed up fifteen minutes late. I suspected she didn't really have a job. I guess she lied about that, too.

My life was the same routine every day; get up, work on saving Sammy's money, fight off creditors, grab a bite to eat, go back to the hole, and try to avoid Monster Woman and Lucy. Then one day Sammy's lawyer called and said there was a bankruptcy hearing the following day where they would discuss the fact that the creditors wanted to put a receiver in place. That's when the court appoints a trustworthy person to handle and manage the money. I was a little worried about that because that was my job. The difference was that I made sure Sammy's employees got taken care of first. I was not sure if the creditors could care less. I thought, "Well, we will see what happens tomorrow. First, I have to get by another night in the hole." The only thing I had to look forward to was the cute guy in the parking lot. I pulled up and there he was again. He flirted with me a little more this time, but I could not do the forbidden fruit thing again.

Next morning, I wanted to get there as early as possible to prepare for the hearing. I needed to double check that I had the payroll listed, so everyone could get paid including me. We arrived at eleven as did the lawyer for the creditors and the judge. We spent hours going over the business and the debts. We couldn't get to everything so we agreed to come back the next day. I was glad it didn't go too long because I didn't want to be late - or I should say, I *could not* be late. I left and went back to my routine: flirt in the parking lot, piss in the cup and watch Lucy snort smuggled cocaine up her nose.

Next morning, same thing - out by seven, hearing at nine. Three hours into the hearing everyone was fighting over the money. Who should be responsible? The judge made a decision. He made the lawyer the receiver for the creditors. That was bad for Sammy because it meant he would lose control so I argued that it wasn't fair. I think

Sammy's lawyer was sleeping. The next thing I knew the judge appointed me as co-receiver. Sammy and I were a little stunned knowing where I slept every night. Don't people do their homework? He should have known I was under indictment for fraud and yet he appointed me co-receiver.

Life was great!

Chapter 18
THE APARTMENT BUILDING

I had become friends with Sammy's intern, Barry. We shared an interest in real estate. He and I talked a lot about how South Beach was going art deco and how it had attracted developers who paid big money for old hotels and apartment buildings and were turning a profit fairly quickly. I wished Sammy could hold on so he could take advantage of the trend. Barry would bring a foreclosure list to work and we would go over it, wishing we could get into something; but I only had 5K, and he had nothing.

Driving to my hole one day, I saw a FOR SALE sign on a really cute building on 9th and Jefferson. I wrote down the number to call the next day. As I pulled in to the parking lot, Cute Guy was waiting for me. I was flattered. Actually, he had become a fun little distraction. I figured I had nothing to lose. It was just someone to interest me enough to help pass the time. He introduced himself as Mike. Naturally, the first question I asked him was what he was in for. And, predictably, he told me it was for drug trafficking. We exchanged stories for the rest of the time we had. We said good night and made plans to meet at the same place, same time the next day.

Back to the familiar evening nuisance: Monster Woman at the door with the cup. You'd think I would be used to it after four weeks, but it still took me at least forty minutes to pee. She was exceptionally mean that evening. She was spitting nails, as if she was jealous and wanted me to screw up so I could be sent away or have my privileges revoked. As I sat there quietly on the toilet waiting for the pee to arrive she repeated every rule searching for one that I might have broken... So I just took whatever she threw at me and I went to bed. I was so excited to go to work and drive by that cute little apartment building that I woke up before the alarm. "My building" looked vacant. This was a good sign; maybe the owners were desperate to sell. I got to the hotel, quickly ran upstairs to my office and called the number. The voice of a very old man answered. I told him I was interested in his building and asked for the details. He told me it had been vacant for some time and needed a lot of repairs. He had a mortgage on the property that was assumable. I requested a tour of the property right away. We set it for three o'clock and I could hardly wait. Meanwhile, I had a lot of work to do for Sammy, had to be in the hole by five p.m. and was suppose to meet the Cute Parking Lot Guy at four-thirty. Busy day! I told Sammy about my plan and he was cool with it so he let me leave a little early.

Pulling up to the front of the building, I could see it being mine. "My place" had a presence about it. There were four floors, ten apartments on each - some were studios and some were one-bedrooms. Each apartment had hardwood floors and a real fireplace. It was so cute. The floors needed to be stripped and repaired. The walls needed paint and some windows needed to be restored. Overall it wasn't too bad. I could fix it up in no time. Next, I had to see if I could afford it. The old man told me that he wanted thirty thousand; plus assuming the mortgage. I offered him fifteen thousand. We agreed at twenty. I called Barry, the intern, right away and told him about the deal thinking he would agree to split it with me. He told me he didn't have any money. I said neither did I, but maybe we could raise it. He chickened out.

All excited about my project, I went back to my hole and forgot about Parking Lot Guy. He was still outside waiting for me so I trotted downstairs. We had fifteen minutes. I was beginning to like him more and more. He was really funny and quite nice. When he made me laugh, I would forget about all the things in my head for just those fleeting minutes. We decided to meet again the next day - same time, same place. Where else, right?

I could hardly sleep. The apartment was calling me. It was perfect. I would work very hard to get it up to par. Ideas were swirling.

If only I weren't in jail.

That morning I called Jerry hoping he would get as excited about my building as I was. We made arrangements to meet there just before I had to go back to the hole. He brought my mother along and they both loved it. He saw the potential right away and confirmed my hope that there was a lot of money to be made when it was all rented. We talked about all the work I would have to put into it before it was ready.

My mother got enthusiastic, too. This was new behavior. She wanted in and thought she could get my brother Ivan to invest, as well. I had the five thousand and I needed fifteen. I would put it together and I would pay Ivan back the difference after we sold it or got it fully occupied. Ivan was a valet, parking cars. He kept every dollar he ever made - unlike me. Good old Ivan had a lot of cash.

The seller and myself and my mother agreed. She spoke for Ivan. I quickly called Barry to get the papers going, as I had to leave to go back to my hole. Well, my day was now complete - running the hotels, the bankruptcy, the code violations and now an empty apartment building... before five p.m. when I served my sentence.

I pulled into the parking lot where Cutie had hidden flowers in his car for me. It was against the rules to fraternize with the men but next thing I knew he threw me up against the car in the back of the parking lot and kissed me. I knew we were limited and it couldn't go much further than that, but I didn't care. It was still fun and I would take it for what it was: entertainment. Besides, it was a nice topper to an amazing day.

Time to report to Monster and the cup. I couldn't understand it. Every test had been clean for months. Why would she waste her time every single night? But this evening I was floating on air. I had hope for my future. I only had to endure two more months in the hole, so I would pleasantly pee for the old bag as much as she demanded. On this particular night, I was so excited it took longer to concentrate on releasing my urine. I started chatting with her and I couldn't contain my enthusiasm. I shared about my new project. Monster was not happy about that. She told me she would have to tell Dan, my probation officer, because I was forbidden do anything on my own or do any business like that while being in jail. Damn. She was going to make sure the authorities knew what I was up to. She said that I would most likely have to give it back. When she got done lecturing me, I felt like she had thrown me off a building. I had gone from cloud nine to sub zero in thirty seconds. I handed the cup to a very smug monster and went upstairs to try to sleep.

That next morning, I arrived at the building as early as I could. I was not about to let Monster ruin my plans. I was making a concise list of all the repairs that were needed. When walking through the basement of the building, I found a tall, skinny, tattooed man sleeping under a blanket next to the boiler. He frightened me. I quickly ran upstairs, got in my car and drove off to work. Good thing Sammy's hotel was only a few blocks away. I was concerned about the man in the basement. I didn't know how I was going to get rid of him and yet at the same time I felt sorry for him. I wondered how long he had been there and if he had any food.

When I got to the hotel, my head was spinning. How was I going to get the money even to buy paint? And who would paint it? And how much could I get done in between all my Sammy duties and trying to make it back to the hole in time? And what else was the monster going to do to sabotage me?

Luckily, I had made a deal with the mortgage holder that I did not have to make payments on my building for ninety days. That gave me a little time to get the repairs going. Some of the employees at the hotel were getting nervous about their jobs and their pay, since we were in receivership. A girl named Linda was working in housekeeping. She was in charge of the cleaning people and was living at the hotel in exchange for some of her pay. It was a good arrangement at the time, but it would soon be over. She was a reliable employee, so I thought I could make her the same deal at my new building. Obviously, I couldn't be living there to run it, so she seemed to be the perfect solution.

During her lunch hour I took her to see my new venture and she loved it. I told her I would give her a commission for every apartment she rented and she could have hers for free as long as she painted and repaired it herself. Then I told her to offer each potential tenant sixty days free rent in lieu of repairs they did themselves. I would personally inspect the progress of each tenant's work and Linda would manage the building until I got out.

The first tenant was the bum in the basement. It made more sense to me that we offer him a deal as opposed to trying to put him out on the street. His name was José, he was from Puerto Rico and he didn't speak much English. I think he had been living in the basement for quite some time. We offered him a cozy apartment as long as he would paint the inside of the building and make some small repairs. I would also help him with food and clothing. He seemed very grateful. I scraped together a few hundred dollars with that week's check and bought paint. Within a week we were able to put a sign outside for rent.

I spent my days driving back and forth from the hotel to the apartment building. Every morning I had to have all the money and reports for the hotels ready to bring to the creditors' office for a full accounting by eleven. I had to juggle the code violations because there was no money for repairs and the hotels were very close to being sold. I needed extensions. I went to a hearing and the judge granted me another fifteen days. It wasn't much but better than nothing. I was worried that the judge would find out where I was sleeping at night but, if he didn't know, I certainly was not going to tell him. After my long/short day I would rush back to the hole stopping first to make out with my cute parking lot boy behind the dumpster for a few minutes. I called it my stress release.

Monster Lady was waiting for me at the door with a real attitude. While I sat on the toilet, she told me she had discussed my situation with my probation officer and that, just as she had suspected (hoped), I had broken the rules. I should have asked him before I did anything and I needed the court's permission to make any changes regarding my standard work release permit. I could tell she had enjoyed her little fact-finding expedition. She informed me that Dan would be visiting the next day and I would probably have my work release program stripped. And then she added, "Since you broke the rules, you'll likely be leaving my facility and going to the Women's Penitentiary." She moved closer to me, her strong arms crossed, squinted her eyes and wagged her head like a bully on the playground. She loved the moment a little too much.

I sat there quietly and took it. I handed over the plastic cup and went to my personal hole. Damn her. She hated me from the moment I arrived. Would she rather I had no job or ambition and stay in the house all day and eat the three free meals and live off the system like everyone else there? I could not understand it.

That morning, when I stopped at the building on my way to the hotel, Linda told me a guy named Dan had been there the day before and had said that he was my probation officer. I was shocked. I couldn't believe he would tell the general public about my personal stuff. She was nervous about my situation and said he had been asking all kinds of questions. This was not good at all. Then she told me she had already rented four apartments and was hoping her hard work was not for nothing. I assured her that everything would be all right. I was not sure I believed it myself but it sounded good.

When I arrived at the hotel, the front desk said there was a guy wandering around asking everyone questions about me. What was Dan doing? Why wasn't he being discreet? I wanted to smack him, but I knew I had better keep my cool or he could pull my plug.

I saw him coming out of Sammy's office.

Oh god. What had he done?

Since Sammy knew everything it wasn't as threatening as it might have been, but what if Dan had told him I was going away? I was a wreck. I got the sweaty palms again.

I got my act together and brought Dan upstairs to my office. He was walking around with the piss cup in his hand the whole time. The first thing he did was hand it to me and followed me to the bathroom. He stood outside the door to make sure I was not exchanging my urine with someone else's. He then asked me about my apartment house business. I nicely explained to him that it had been my understanding that I was not allowed to make any telephone sales. I clarified my concept and how it was just my brother who was putting up the money and that it was supposed to be an investment for our future. I hoped he saw that instead of going the way of crime or drugs, I was making myself useful and preparing for a lawful way of life once I got out.

Dan didn't seem to care. He hated me, too. He said I better hope my pee was clean. What exactly did I do to make him detest me? I had been amenable and cooperative - and clean. He went on to say he was sending a letter to the judge for him to make a decision. I could only imagine how he would slant the facts. He stayed there for at least two hours of interrogation and torture. That put me so behind in my day; I was almost late for my receivership reports. I never mentioned to Dan about me being co-receiver. That might not have gone so well.

With very little time left in the hole, I was getting excited. I was also thrilled because the apartment was filling up and it was starting to look like a real place.

My mother called, badgering me about the return on Ivan's money. Neither of them had even come by the place to help or to see all the improvements. They also did not understand the concept of having the tenants do the work in lieu of rent money for sixty days. I tried to explain that we had received a ninety-day reprieve before any payments were due. It was all going just as planned. But Mom was anxious - she wanted the money for Ivan right then. That's when I suspected she might not have told Ivan he was an apartment landlord. That just added to the pressure on top of the rest of the crap that was going down.

For the first time I was scared to return to the hole. What if Dan the Probation Man and his best friend Monster Woman got together and ganged up on me to make sure I went to the penitentiary? I had such a bad feeling about my day. Why was he asking so many questions?

I got to the hole with enough time to see my parking lot boy. He was so cute that day. Maybe it was in contrast to all the ugly people I had been dealing with. He gave me a pleasant little diversion by making out in his car for twenty minutes. I asked him if he was having similar problems in the hole or with his probation. Since he was in there for drug trafficking I figured he must have been really harassed. He said that they had only drug tested him once when he arrived. That was it. I could not believe it. It just confirmed how much the monster hated me.

Our time was over and we went inside. Same old routine: cup time followed by berating time. Were they trying to drive me crazy so I would be frustrated enough to do drugs and finally fail the test? Was that her evil plan? Well, it wasn't going to work. I had little time left to make my millions and this crazy system with its evil personnel was not going to get in my way.

When I got to my room, there were three big policewomen tearing the room apart while Lucy was handcuffed to the chair. I was so scared that she might have put some of her stuff on my side. After twenty minutes of searching, they found a bag of cocaine and some pills taped to the inside of the toilet bowl. There were also tubes of urine taped to the back of the toilet. Thank god somehow they knew this was all Lucy's. The police came and took Lucy away to another place.

I had a horrible night. Between my mom and Dan and the stupid monster woman, the burden was getting to me. And then all the hotel inspectors, and trying to get the hotels sold before we could be cited for more expensive problems, and the whole thing about the judge not knowing I was convicted and living in a detention center, and all the work I was doing trying not to let Sammy down. It was all piling up, but I would be damned if I was going to let anxiety stop me. I had a good idea with this apartment building and no one was going to prevent me from getting my well deserved fortune. I was twenty-two. I still had time. I finally fell asleep as the sun was rising.

A few hours later I got to my apartment building, not knowing what to expect. Linda came running out and told me she rented out six more apartments! The timing could not have been better. I only had to rent half the building in order to cover the mortgage and it looked like that might be happening before the first payment was due.

José, the bum-from-the-basement-turned-painter, was actually doing a good job. He was a very hard worker but he never spoke. I told him I appreciated his work and congratulated Linda on the great job she was doing. Then I quickly left for my real job.

My first call of the day was to my mother. She wanted a full accounting. She was complaining that we had purchased the building almost two months ago and demanded an explanation as to why there was no money for Ivan. I begged her to come down and see all the improvements. I told her it would help tremendously if she would come and help me paint because I didn't have much time. She declined.

For the rest of the month it was the same old story: the bankruptcy, code violations, apartment buildings, Cute Parking Lot Boy, Dan the Probation Man and Monster Lady. With only two weeks to go at my residence I was being extra cooperative. We had heard nothing from Dan's report to the judge. It was countdown and I was being very careful. I just wanted to go quietly away. I was making big plans with Jerry. He was telling me about all these projects he was interested in and I could not wait to be a part of it. Unfortunately, my Parking Lot Boy sessions would be ending because he still had two months left. Oh well. I remained grateful for the distraction.

Five days to release date and I was doing my routine. First, I checked on Linda. She had rented two more. This was going amazingly well. Next, Sammy's sales of two of the hotels were going through. My job was winding down. I only had to wrap up my last code violations so there would be nothing against the property. The final hearing was happening the week after my release. The relentless worry was becoming more manageable. I was looking forward to my new freedom.

Linda called and asked me to come by because she was having a problem with José. Apparently he was drunk and was throwing bottles at passing cars from the roof. I told her I would be right there. This was a bit of a pain, but nothing I couldn't handle.

I pulled up and spotted him on the roof. I yelled for him to get down. He yelled back something about how I was not paying him enough money. He sounded extremely intoxicated. I was afraid to call the cops because they would probably arrest him and take him away -- I preferred trying to help him. I'd call 911 instead.

I went into Linda's apartment to use the phone. As I was waiting for them to answer, José stormed through the door, walked right up to me and struck me in the chest. I didn't know what happened. I fell to the floor and saw deep red blood emerging. That's when I looked up and saw the seven-inch fishing knife. Oh god. He was crazed. He raised his hand again. I panicked as I saw the wet blade coming back at me. I tried to defend myself by grabbing it, struggling to prevent it from reaching my chest again. I had no power over this insane beast. The knife cut deeply into my hand and severed my fingers. He continued slashing me. I was fighting for my life.

I heard the faint voice of 911 on the phone near the table.

"Hello? What's going on in there?"

I could not respond. I was taking the blade over and over again while José was telling me he loved me. He was intent on puncturing my heart but I kept grabbing the knife to soften the insertion. My hand was mutilated. There was so much slippery blood all around I feared I was doomed to bleed to death. My middle finger was gone and my others were helplessly dangling, so I started kicking. He stabbed me in the legs, butt and almost removed my left nipple. At one point I wrestled the knife away with my good hand. Just as that happened the old neighbor lady came in and hit him over the head with a chair. With one arm, he threw her across the room like bag of garbage. She ran out.

"Hello? Hello? What's going on? This is 911. What's happening?"

I was very weak but I was not going to let him win. I had come too far. I still had the knife in my other hand but José was on top of me. He yanked the cord to the air conditioner out of the wall and wrapped it around my neck and started choking me. He retrieved his weapon and stabbed me a few more times until I passed out. I am not sure if I did that to make him think I was dead, but it worked.

He got up from where I lay and walked out the door.

Chapter 19
TWO HUNDRED STITCHES

I was not sure if I was dead or not. I went in and out of consciousness... neighbors staring, deep red blood on everything, ambulance noises, policemen, and my finger lying next to my left hand. *Black.* I could not tell where all the pain was coming from. It was everywhere, like a loud siren. I didn't see Linda. It was unclear, but I remembered that she had left me inside with him. It was not her fault. *Black.*

I arrived at the trauma center at Mt. Sinai and came to. The emergency room director asked if I had some family to call. I could barely speak. I whispered Jerry's and my mother's phone numbers to a concerned person. I was crying for Sammy. The nurse called him for me. I was begging him to come. I could tell he was giving her excuses. He was not coming. I then heard the nurse calling my mother. No answer, so she left a message. They only had one name left. The nurse called Jerry. At that point I was screaming while they were sewing my finger back on.

Apparently, while the nurse was on the phone with Jerry, he was on the other line with my mother. Mom had called Jerry instead of the emergency room because it was a long distance call even though Jerry was long distance, too. She told him to find out what happened and to call her back. He hung up and drove to the hospital.

In the trauma unit, they were sewing me back together - over two hundred stitches. I was still in shock but quite alert after they finished. My body was trembling uncontrollably and my teeth were chattering. Jerry walked in. I was so happy to see someone. He pretended that I looked fine and that everything would be okay. I could tell he was worried, though. Although I had not seen myself in the mirror, I knew that they had put stitches in almost every part of my small body.

In a weak, breathless voice, I asked Jerry when my mother was coming. He said she was waiting for him to call to tell what had happened and how I was. I could tell by the tone in his voice he was not pleased with her response. He stayed with me for about twenty-five minutes. During that time he said, "You're going to be just fine" about twenty-five times. I didn't care. I was just happy to have someone at my side.

After many hours in the trauma ward, the doctor came in and closed the door. He had a regretful look in his eyes that worried me. He began with, "I'm sorry to tell you..."

I was thinking, "What could he be sorry about? I'm alive! What else could be wrong?"

"I'm afraid you experienced some severe nerve damage to your left arm and your middle finger. I can't say at this point if you will ever have normal function - if any - to your arm. You will need extensive rehabilitation and you will have to stay hooked up to a nerve stimulator every day."

My only reaction was, "Well, that's still better than the alternative."

The next visitors were two police officers. The first thing I asked was why 911 didn't answer the phone and why it took so long for them to get there. They didn't have a comment to that. They were just there to investigate a crime. One of the officers then said, "I notice in the report that you are currently residing in the Dade County corrections facility."

"Yes, and would you please call them? I think I'm going to be late." I had no idea how many hours had passed. I didn't want to jeopardize my chances of getting released on time.

They looked at each other and then the skinny one asked a barrage of questions, "What were you doing in that old building? Was this a drug deal gone wrong? Are you a prostitute? What did you do to provoke him?" I couldn't answer any of them. I was still traumatized, in acute pain, dazed and confused. Their questions were not only offensive but made no sense to me.

A call came over their radio saying that José had been apprehended. He had walked right up to the police cruiser still holding the seven-inch fishing knife covered in my blood and openly admitted what he'd done. Apparently still intoxicated, he rambled to the police, "I killed the bitch. I hope she is dead. She's charging too much rent. Is the bitch dead yet? Did I kill her?" I was told that he repeated those words over and over.

No, I was *not* dead.

The officers continued to interrogate me for hours even though the nurse told them that I needed to get my strength back. She was right. The adrenalin that had kept me alert was slowing down and the pain was taking over. They kept asking me questions as if I was the criminal, not the victim. I couldn't understand why they were so mean to me. They warned me that they would be back for further questions, and then they finally left.

About ten hours later, the nice nurses wheeled me upstairs to a room. Jerry, who had been waiting in the hallway, came right behind. He stayed with me until I fell asleep. I felt a little safer with him by my side.

The sound of my own screams woke me from my drug induced sleep. The nurses came running in to see what was wrong. I was out of my mind with pain and trauma. I kept screaming, "Make him stop! Make him stop!"

The nurse told me I was dreaming and that she was going to medicate me so I could rest. Within a minute I was asleep again.

136

Searing pain and harsh reality were waiting for me the next morning. The story slowly came back - I was in the hospital with over two hundred stitches because José went crazy on me. My body throbbed in the most indescribable way.

I hadn't wanted to go back to the hole, but *this* was not what I had in mind. With consciousness came worrisome questions. What if those officers thought I did something wrong? What if I had to start my sentence all over again? What was going to happen to the hotels? My mind spiraled and my body ached. The worst pain was coming from my finger. I screamed for the nurse. She arrived quickly with more pain medication. She then told me the doctor would be in to see me in a little while. I asked her how long I would have to stay there. She didn't answer me.

The pain medicine was very strong. I could hardly focus. I couldn't decide if this was a good or bad thing. I'm a fighter and I know how to call upon my strength, but the medication kept me in a fog. I had to trust that my subconscious would keep the fire in me burning.

There was a light knock on the door. I struggled to open my eyes and thought I saw Avi. Was I dreaming? No, he had come to see me. He shared the same look on his face that Jerry had in the emergency room. It was a combination of horror, pity and sympathy. He didn't stay long because it was obvious I was not up for conversation. He just wanted me to know he was there for me. He kissed me in between the stitches on my forehead and then he left. That was about the best medicine I could have gotten.

I fell asleep for a little while and was woken up by the doctor examining every stitch to see his work. He looked pleased. I told him of the horrendous pain in my finger. He looked at me and started to smile. I didn't get it. I was in pain and this doctor was smiling? I asked why. With his very deep voice he said he had been afraid that I had lost all the nerves in my arm and that it might never work again. They thought they would possibly have to remove the entire arm. Hearing that, I realized that the pain was perfect. I found a way to put a positive spin into the equation, but it still hurt like hell. The doctor wrote some notes on my chart and said he would see me the next day.

Jerry called on the phone to see how I was. I told him what the doctor had said and he also found the excitement. I asked him about my mother and when she might be coming. He reported that I was to call her when I needed a ride home and that she would gladly pick me up. I told him I didn't know when that would be, but I would call. I was not surprised. My mother wasn't a nurturer. I was going to have to be on my own to heal. She offered to do a dutiful thing - pick me up. That was about all she could muster up. I just hoped that she wasn't going to rag on me about Ivan's money.

Barry, the intern, was the next to visit. He said he was sorry he got me involved in real estate. I asked him about the hearing. It had happened that morning and he had gone on my behalf. The judge had not been happy about that. Not because we had failed some inspections or anything, but because Barry told the judge that I was not his partner. He informed the judge that I was the manager of the hotels and worked for Sammy. The judge angrily said that I had been impersonating a lawyer, that he was going to hold me in contempt of court and that I was never to step into his courtroom again. Barry tried to calm him down so we didn't blow all our motions to dismiss. The judge later assessed a fine and slammed his hammer down and said NEXT. I guess the end result was okay. I couldn't believe what bad luck I had with judges. Actually, the bad luck came when someone else spoke in my place. *There* was the lesson.

Barry saw that I was getting tired. He said good-by and snuck out of the room.

The pain medicine was wearing off and the unbearably thick knife cuts were throbbing. I had to yell for the nurse. She came quickly with her needle. I got so dizzy when the cold liquid went through my veins. I was starting to understand what it felt like to get high. It was not for me at all. I did not like the sensation of not knowing which way was up or down. My head spun around until I fell asleep. The drugs only lasted about four to five hours. Once I was asleep and the medicine wore off, I would fall into horrifying nightmares of that skinny tattooed man chasing me with a fishing knife.

Sammy called. I still could not understand why he hadn't come to see me. He couldn't be *that* busy. I begged to see him and then he finally admitted that he had a bad thing about hospitals. He didn't explain it, but he said he hated hospitals. He assured me that he would make sure I would have the best care he could get. I really wanted to see him, but I guess I understood.

Laura and Joey came the following day. They were so concerned. I had not seen her since I went to the hole. She looked good -- Joey was the same. Laura had moved back to her mom's in Miami while I was away. It didn't seem like they were seeing each other as much but what did I know? I was so high on meds. I was hoping Laura didn't know what was in the IV. She might have taken it for herself. They leaned over my bed, gave me a kiss good-bye and said they would see me soon.

If I made the tiniest move, it felt as if I was going to die of the pain. Whenever the drugs wore off I was on fire. The longer I lay there, the worse I felt. I even had stitches in my butt and I was lying right on them. It felt like I was ripping them out every time I stirred.

When the doctor came in to see me I begged him to let me go home. I needed to get back to my life. He said that when I was able to walk by myself he would consider it. I told him to move and I would get up and walk. I wasn't sure I could do it, but I sure would die trying. I slid to the side and put my injured legs to the floor. I didn't have use of either of my arms. They were both wrapped up tight and the left one was set closed to my chest. As I was trying to find my balance, it became clear to me how bad off I really was. How could I take care of myself when I couldn't even wipe myself? I didn't care. I would figure it out.

I held my breath so the doctor wouldn't see the pain in my face and I struggled to put one foot in front of the other. He was pleased. He said he would release me later that day, but that I must go to rehab.

Wait one minute. What was I doing? Where was I going? Did I need to go back to the hole? Was the monster lady waiting for me? How would I pass her drug test? How would I drive with no arms? Who was going to help me in the apartment?

I had never needed help like this before. My sense of independence was extremely compromised and I hated it. I had no clear reason to trust that people would help me when I needed it.

First, I had to call Dan, my probation officer. I was hoping he had heard where I had been. I prayed he hadn't put a warrant out for me. I managed to walk over to the phone on the desk by the door. I pushed the handle off the receiver with a couple of fingers on my right hand and put it on speaker phone. Luckily I remembered his number.

He answered in his old cranky voice. I told him I was still in the hospital but that they were going to release me. I asked him if I had done my time from my sentence because this was the day of my scheduled release date. He said he was sorry about what had happened to me but added that I must have done something to make my perpetrator mad. The only good thing that came out of his mouth was he had discussed my situation with the judge and was told that the court had considered that my time spent in the hospital was time spent in the hole and I was released. However, I had to report to his probation office once a week and needed to start my community service. I also had to keep working to repay the fine. I was happy about these conditions. I told him I would see him at the end of the week.

Next, I talked to Sammy to see if I still had a job now that I was a bit handicapped. He said of course, and that he would pick me up the next morning. He then reported that Linda had been calling him every day. She had told him she felt so guilty about what had happened to me that she wanted to make up for it by living with me and helping me until I got back on my feet. I was happy to hear that, especially since I didn't have any other offers.

My next call was to my mother. I told her I would be ready within the hour and I would appreciate it if she would pick me up. She asked me how I was feeling. I didn't really know how to answer that although I was glad she asked. I could never guess what mood mom would be in and the question had caught me a little off guard.

After we hung up I noticed I didn't have any clothes to wear for my release, so I called my mother back and asked her to bring me something very loose to wear.

I then called Jerry and told him I was leaving the hospital and that I was officially released from the Women's Correctional Center. I added that I was hoping he hadn't forgotten all the deals we had agreed to work on as soon as I got out of the hole. He hadn't.

About two hours later, my nurse came in to tell me my mother was outside and that I was free to go. She gave me some pain pills to take so I could survive the car ride. I thanked her sincerely and gave her a hug goodbye. She had been a nurturing figure in an otherwise lonely place. After all, I was about to see my own mother for the first time since I had been brutally attacked.

The nurse pushed the wheelchair out to the curb. I was a little nervous to see my mother. I didn't know what she was going to say. She helped me into the car and I think she was a little shocked that I was hurt so badly. Maybe she felt a little guilty. I could only hope.

She started to drive toward my townhouse, which I had not seen for nearly six months. She drove so fast I could feel every little bump. It was excruciating. I begged her to slow down to least avoid the bumps. She accommodated me.

We arrived at my little house where Linda was waiting. She met me at the driveway and carefully helped me out of the car. My mother hung around for a few minutes. She did not seem at all interested in what was under all my bandages. I told Mom I had to go to therapy and that I would appreciate it if she could take me. She agreed to take me all though by the look on her face it was a big inconvenience for her I think as long as I was alive I must be fine.

I moved slowly around the house trying to familiarize myself. I looked to the left and saw the giant staircase to the bedroom. I had been longing for a real bed instead of that thin, squeaky cot, six inches off the floor I had been sleeping on for the last six months. The stairs looked impossible. With Linda's help, I took each step with a deep breath, a wince of unbearable pain and pure determination. Once I made it to the top I realized I had to use the bathroom for the first time since they removed the catheter. Good thing I was used to peeing in public. Linda kindly cleaned me up, walked me to the bed, put the phone near me and sat next to me until I fell asleep.

Halfway through the night, I was awakened by the ringing of the phone. When I answered there was a deep voice on the other side saying, "WHY AREN'T YOU DEAD? YOU ARE SUPPOSED TO BE DEAD!" I threw the phone down and started screaming. Linda came running. She told me it was okay, that I was dreaming just like I had done in the hospital. She gave me some of my magic pills and I dizzily fell back to sleep.

The next morning I woke up a little confused about my whereabouts and was still trying to figure out what had happened with the phone in the middle of the night.

I was scheduled for therapy. It sounded very painful. At this point there wasn't a time when I was pain free. At best, and with medication, it was a constant low-grade throb. Something as simple as turning to my side to sleep was a huge challenge with agonizing consequences. Sitting was impossible. The idea of going to therapy was upsetting to say the least.

Linda found a loose fitting dress in the closet and put it on me. Little by little we made our way downstairs. The pain was horrendous. Linda gave me another magic pill so I could handle the ride and the therapy. She then carefully placed me into Mom's car and off the three of us went to the first of what would be many weeks of therapy.

A nice lady was waiting for me at the rehab center. She told Mom and Linda to wait in the reception area while she took me back to remove my bandages.

I had not yet seen my ravaged body. Stitches were everywhere and it felt like each one was being ripped out as she gradually pulled the bandages away from my skin. My left arm was the worst. Near my elbow the knife had entered the front and exited the back. Half of that arm was extremely painful and the other half had no feeling whatsoever. The enormity of seeing my destroyed arm made the whole scenario more intense. This produced even more pain. As if that realization wasn't enough, I still said yes when she asked me if I was sure I wanted to see myself in a mirror. I looked like something out of a horror movie. José had been prolific. I reminded myself once again that it was better than the alternative.

The nice therapist put some cream on my wounds and then took me to a table and had me lie down. She then began this terrible process of moving my very stiff limbs around as I screamed my head off. She said if she didn't do that I would never move anything again.

After that nightmare, she put wires from my chest to my left arm and then to my hand. When she turned the machine on I started trembling. I felt like I was having a heart attack; the nerves in my chest were somehow connected to my arm and it was excruciatingly painful.

Two hours later, I was ready to go home. The nice lady at the counter told me I needed to come four times a week and reminded me to do stretches every day. She added that she was ordering a small machine like the one she had just used on me and I needed to wear it twenty-four hours a day for three months. My first thought was, "I'd rather die."

Linda and my mom were somewhat patient. Linda carefully placed me in the car. I wanted to see Sammy but I just didn't have the strength.

Heading for home I was so worried about getting my life back together. It seemed impossible. I asked my mother if she had gone by the apartment building to see what had been happening. Of course she hadn't, but she started ragging on me about Ivan's money. I had no answer for her. Then she informed me that she couldn't take me to therapy the rest of the week because she had to work. Linda told her not to worry - she would drive me in my car. Since she didn't have a car and that's why mom agreed to drive in the first place.

Once inside the house, the top of the stairs looked so far away as if I had to climb a mountain. I was exhausted and in deep pain from the ordeal, so Linda gave me another magic pill in order to help me get up my staircase. My body felt exposed without the bandages. Each step took amazing amounts of concentration. When I got to the top the phone was ringing. Linda answered it and no one was on the other end, so she hung up.

The best news the therapist had given me was that I could finally take a shower. I couldn't wait to get all the dried up blood that covered my small frame washed off. *Maybe I won't look so bad when I'm all cleaned up.* As I stood under the water, the tub became red. It was a strange sensation of soothing warmth and prickly pain, but the idea of getting clean was so satisfying I stayed there until I ran out of hot water.

I put on a hospital gown since it was the only loose thing I had and climbed into bed. I called Sammy to see if he would pick me up the next day. I was ready! He was happy to hear my voice and could not wait to see me.

Lying in bed, my head was spinning. Those magic pills were very strong. I tried to focus on the ceiling to make the room stop. The phone rang again. I answered and it was the same deep voice, "WHY AREN'T YOU DEAD?" The voice lowered to almost a whisper, "I will kill you next time." I threw the phone to the floor and screamed. I wasn't crazy - this was really happening. Or was it the pills? By the time Linda came in I wasn't sure anymore. I left the phone off the hook and fell asleep. I decided not to take any more pills, no matter how bad the pain was. They were going to drive me crazy.

I woke up with excitement. Sammy was coming! I was going to the hotel to put my life back together. My enthusiasm was met with blazing pain. I hadn't taken a magic pill for twelve hours. I was used to taking them every four hours, but I was determined not to let the painkillers take over my life. And I didn't want Sammy to think I was in La-La Land. I had to suck it up.

He pulled up to the driveway and Linda helped me get into his car. My arms weren't bandaged anymore, and though they weren't tied down, they still didn't work very well. He gave me a much-needed, gentle hug. I noticed that he had that same pitying look on his face that Jerry and Avi had when they saw me. His eyes avoided me when he spoke. I was trying to understand. I probably looked like a monster.

We arrived at the hotel and some of the employees were outside waiting for me. They were so happy to see me. I got out of the car and tried to hide my face so they wouldn't see the pain. When was it going to subside?

I spent a few hours trying to pick up where I had left off. Barry had handled the code violations. One hotel deal had closed, which meant that Jerry had made a bunch of money. I called the lawyers in the receivership to see if everything was okay. They were just glad to know I was doing all right and even offered me a job when the rest of the hotels were sold. They didn't know what kind of job, but said they would figure that out. Hmmm... I guess they didn't know where I had been sleeping while handling all that money.

I was getting tired and the pain was getting worse, but I wanted to go to the apartment building just for a minute. Sammy could see I needed my rest and he didn't want me going there by myself so he had his driver, Felix, take me. I needed to face it. I had to go and check on Ivan's money.

As we pulled up to the building I froze for a moment, but quickly forced myself to get it together. One of the tenants, an old lady, was outside sweeping. She came running to the car to help me. She took me inside and wanted to mother me. She filled me in on what had happened after the incident. She said everyone but she had moved out in fear. The good thing was all the

146

apartments were in better shape than when the tenants had first moved in.

I walked to apartment number five - the scene of the crime, determined to face the horrible memory head on. I'd be damned if I was going to let pain - either physical or emotional - stand in the way of my ability to move my life forward. I stood there with my stitched up hand quivering on the doorknob, trying to muster up the strength to go inside. I had to remind myself of my mantra - that this trauma, as terrifying as it was, was better than the alternative. That gave me the courage to open the door.

My eyes immediately focused on the corner of the room near the desk and the phone. Why couldn't the 911 operators hear my anguish over the phone? I focused on a dark area on the floor; my blood soaked in the wood. I had to fight the screams that wanted to come out. Instead, I asked the old lady if she had something to help me clean it up. She told me she would take care of it. I said I would do it myself as had to be the one to put myself back together and this task was a symbol of all the work I had to face to get back on track. I was not about to let two hundred stitches get in the way of being a whole person again. I still had my sights on becoming a millionaire.

I found some paint thinner in the closet and poured it on the floor. I couldn't bend down, so I rubbed it with a mop. Each stroke was as painful as it was cathartic. A lot of it came up so I poured on a little more thinner and continued dragging the mop over the stain. It was going to be okay. I told the old lady I would be back in a few days. I had exhausted myself and it was time for me to go home.

When I told Linda I had gone to the apartment building she was upset. When she heard I had cleaned my own blood up, she became furious. She had already paid someone out of her own money to make sure I never had to see that horrible stain.

It had been almost twenty-four hours since I had taken my last painkiller and I was getting used to the constant aching and throbbing. I was well aware though that the next day I would have to go back to physical therapy and I dreaded the nice lady and her torture machine.

I carefully pulled myself up the stairs to take a long, hot shower. It was an amazing experience to let the warm water flow over all my cuts and bruises. It seemed as if I was washing off the dried blood all over again. I needed a good cleansing after visiting apartment number five. Once again I languished under the gentle faucet until the water turned tepid.

As Linda smoothed the cream into my broken skin, the exhaustion took over. I crawled into bed with immense relief and as I began to drift the phone startled me. I was afraid to answer, so I let it ring and ring and ring. Then I started stressing that it might be important or maybe someone was in trouble - why else would they let it ring so many times? When I finally answered, the deep voice asked, "WHY AREN'T YOU DEAD? I *WILL* KILL YOU." I pulled the phone out of the wall and started crying. Was I crazy? I hadn't had a magic pill in twenty-four hours, so it couldn't be that. It was real. I decided to tell Sammy so he could help me call the police and get my phone number changed. How could he do this to me? José was in jail awaiting his trial, how could he call? Was I suffering from some kind of stress disorder?

I was relieved to see the sun enter my window. It had been a rough night between the pain, the phone and the residual stress of the day before. I was ready to start fresh.

Linda got the car ready and we piled in and drove straight to therapy. The nice lady was there again. She brought me in right away and put me on the table. I closed my eyes in anticipation of the blast of pain. I had not indulged in the magic pills this time and I knew how brutal the session was going to be. She started pulling my stiff legs while I held my breath until she was finished. She then took this small, but powerful-looking, machine out of the box and started installing wires from my chest to my left arm to my hand. It was a smaller version of the killer one she had hooked me up to a couple of days before. This was almost more frightening than when José came at me with his fishing knife. This time I knew how bad it was going to feel and to make matters worse, it was supposed to be attacking me twenty-four hours a day. I barraged her with questions. "How am I going to live with this? How do I shower? How do I get dressed?" She showed me how she had attached the wires with suction cups that allowed me to disconnect when I showered. I was to put them right back on afterward. She told me I must keep it on all day and all night and to keep it set on high. It felt like I was going to have a heart attack.

The nice lady finished hooking me up, scheduled the next appointment and sent me home. Of all the things I had to do to heal myself, this took the most courage. You don't know how badly I wanted to rip out those shock-making wires.

I convinced Linda to take me back to the building so I could check things out and figure out how to get new tenants. The mortgage payments were due in a few days and I didn't have any money to pay them since we lost every potential paying tenant. My mother was driving me crazy about Ivan's money. How was I supposed to give him a return on his money when there wasn't any?

Linda would not go into the building once we got there. She said it brought back too many horrific memories of the stabbing. I thought I was the victim.

The first thing I did was go back to Apartment Five to see if there was any more of "me" left on the floor. It was much better, but it was not perfect. There was a permanent blood stain soaked into the hard wood as a reminder of good intentions gone wrong. I stared at it and all of a sudden I felt as though I was lying there trying to grab the knife before it went into my chest. I saw my finger lying next to my hand. I saw José's crazed face staring wildly as his armed plunged the knife all over my body over and over again. I heard the sound of his breath and the thud of the weapon as it sliced into my flesh.

No wonder Linda didn't want to come in.

The old neighbor lady and her husband offered to replace all the wood. They said it would be very expensive, but they didn't mind doing it. I just didn't have the money. I had *no* money, as a matter of fact. I asked them if they would not mind moving into Apartment Five, as I wouldn't be able to rent it. They were not happy but they agreed as long as the rent was free. I was planning to advertise again and needed them to show the place. They told me the crime had been all over the papers and the evening news, making it one of the most undesirable places to rent. People were afraid. I told them to be positive, put on a happy smile, reduce the rent and do whatever it took to get people in there. The old lady was grateful that I was going to keep trying. She didn't want to lose her free place to live. Because I made a deal with her that she could live free if she rent's apartments.

After a long day of exhausting events, we returned home to find my mother waiting at my house demanding explanations about Ivan's investment. I explained to her that since I had been a victim of an attempted murder, we had to start all over again with new tenants. I reminded her that this little knifing inconvenience took me away from focusing on replacing the tenants and the mortgage payments were due immediately. With the sympathy of a mob boss, she demanded that I give Ivan back his money immediately or sign all my interest in the building over to her. I reiterated that at the moment I had NO money and suggested that she and Ivan come and help me fix it up so we could rent it. I told her that we could make it work and just needed a little time. She again repeated her demands and threatened that there was no changing her mind. We were at a standoff. Neither one of us was budging. I guess we are going back to silence.

The next thing out of her mouth was, "If you don't sign the building over to me and Ivan, I'll call your probation officer and tell him what's going on with Ivan's investment. I'm sure he'll gladly throw you back in jail." What an understanding, motherly expression of love and caring. She was beginning to outdo the pain machine I was hooked up to. And just as I thought it could not be any more painful, she lowered her voice and said, "What did you do to that man to make him so angry? You must have pissed him off really bad, Gigi, to make him hate you so much."

Shocked and upset, I told her I needed to rest and began my long trek upstairs.

I wasn't sure if we had enough hot water to flush her filth off me.

Chapter 20
FRIENDS AND ENEMIES

My mother left me feeling like I was covered in waste. All I wanted to do was take my shower and let the warm water wash off my mother's cruel words.

First, I had to separate myself from all the complicated wires attached to my arm, chest and hand. I carefully made note of which wire was hooked up where and disconnected them one at a time. It was a huge relief the moment the lightning bolts stopped jolting me. Under the relaxing stream, I appreciated the respite from pain more than ever and nearly cried when the hot water ran out.

Linda yelled up the stairs to see if I needed any help getting hooked back up, but I was determined to figure it out myself. After I was all plugged in, I called Sammy to make sure he was picking me up the next morning at nine. With my tomorrow organized I climbed into bed with wires in tow and attempted to relax. The pain went on and off like contractions.

I stared at the ceiling trying to make sense of my mother. Why must she threaten and try to control me? Why doesn't she have a *little* compassion for her only daughter? Why was she purposefully putting another roadblock to the millions I could see waiting to be made, and were once again slipping further away? It was extremely frustrating.

Exhaustion finally took over and I fell asleep only to be awoken by the phone again. I lay there listening to the sinister ringing and wondered if I was dreaming again. Could it possibly be real? Then I heard Linda answer. She let out a little scream and then said, "Stop calling! Why are you doing this?" I called down asking who was on the phone. She told me it was a wrong number. I forced myself back to sleep thinking of Sammy and going to work the next morning. Unlike most people, work was my sedative. It was the only way I could get my mind off all the negative things.

I woke up tangled in the wires. Linda came in to disconnect me and then helped reconnect. This was a painstaking job of getting everything in its correct order so it could provide the exact amount of electricity throughout the day. Getting dressed over the wires was a challenge unto itself.

I went as fast as I could to get downstairs where Sammy was waiting. He noticed my torture device as he was helping me get in the car. When I explained he tried to make a joke and told me not to get stuck in the rain. It was funny, but I had never thought of that. Now I had electrocution to add to my list of fears.

I told Sammy about the phone calls. He could not believe that José was free enough to torment me. He promised to call the chief of police when we got to the hotel and assured that he would help me get the phone number changed.

Dan, the Probation Man, was waiting for me with his friendly cup when we pulled up. I was worried that my mother had actually made good on her threat to call him. He watched me struggle to get out of the car. He had not yet seen how badly off I was and I thought he would notice the severity of my condition and have a little sympathy. Instead I got, "Jesus Christ, missy. You must have done something mighty bad to get that guy so pissed off." He punctuated his sentence with a whistle and handed me the cup. He then followed me to the bathroom to finish the routine.

I took him up to my office to discuss my future. That's when he told me my mother had, in fact, called and he was going to meet with her later in the week. My heart sank. Would my own mother try to get me back in jail by telling Dan I extorted money from my brother? What good would that be for anyone? Was she capable of being that callous?

He asked about the apartment building and what was going on with that. I told him everything was great but my good fingers were crossed under the table while my other fingers were getting zapped. He reminded me that I must see him again by the end of the week.

After he finally left, I walked over to the cashier to balance the receivables and payables. With only two hotels left, there was not much to do. A few minutes later Sammy walked in with two detectives. He had told them about the phone calls. They asked me some questions and then called the phone company to get the number changed. I felt a little better. They then told me I needed to go the state attorney's office to prosecute José. They explained that because I hung in there and didn't die, José got a break; the maximum sentence was up to twelve years for attempted murder, but if I died, he could have gotten life. They asked me to take a ride with them to positively identify José. It was part of the procedure, even though he had already admitted his crime. I was not sure I was up for that. Just the thought made me shaky. My frequent nightmares were violent yet vague; arms and hands coming at me with brute force, squishy sounds a knife makes when it's plunging into meat, the heavy breathing and bright red blood appearing out of nowhere. But the dreams didn't give me his face. That would be too much. That would make it too real. Sammy could see how uncomfortable I was and kindly went with me over to the jail. Could José have been calling me from jail?

It was still morning and I was already having a challenging day. I slowly made my way into the jail. This time I would be on the other side of the bars. We went to the third floor where the nice detectives took me into a room with a big glass window. They explained that they were going to line up six guys and I needed to point out which one was José. I was shaking and it wasn't the machine. I had sweaty palms and began to worry I might electrocute myself on top of everything else. This whole thing was not good. They assured me he could not see me. I just didn't understand why I had to do this. He already admitted to the cops that he did it. I felt tortured.

The door opened and a line of men came marching in. I identified him right away. My heart was pushing against my chest when I saw the shit-eating grin on his face. I was both terrified and livid at the same time. I wanted to break through the glass and hurt him, yet I was so nervous I kept asking the detectives if he could see me. It looked as though he was staring right at me. He must have sensed that I was standing there. It was the smile of a lunatic and it pierced my soul.

I clearly identified him and the men were sent out. I couldn't let go of the look he had on his face. I didn't feel safe at all. I sat there frozen in my chair. He *knew* I was there. He could see right through me.

I went straight to work. It was my Xanax. Hard work took my mind off everything else. I had received a message from an old friend I had met in LA. His name was Joe and he was a real estate developer. He was in town and heard about the hotels for sale. Maybe I could work a deal to everyone's best interest. Just the idea of being instrumental in my first million-dollar real estate pitch helped me forget about the anguish that was trying to invade my enthusiasm. Within a few hours I was ready for the presentation.

We had already talked the week before so I calmly called Joe to let him know I was ready. It was the calm part that was hard. After all, Joe was hot. And he was a well-known millionaire who lived in Malibu and hung out with a lot of cool celebrities. And there I was in

Florida, hooked up to a torture chamber and looking like a lab experiment. I was scarcely hanging on to an apartment that had a "curse on it" while trying to tolerate a nagging, deceitful mother who was trying to stop me from reaching my true potential. I was nervous, to say the least.

Joe and I made an appointment for the next day after my physical therapy, though I hadn't mentioned my handicap yet. The last time I spoke to him I was on my way to jail... one thing at a time.

Tired and full of pain, I told Sammy about my upcoming appointment. He was excited and quickly ordered Felix to take me home so I could get my rest. I knew Sammy really needed to sell that hotel. He truly didn't want to lose it to the bank.

When I got home Linda told me that Dallas had called and was coming over. That was odd. I thought our relationship had been severed due to her excess use of coke and the fact that Joey had a new girlfriend. Oh well - I could use some friends at that moment. I needed to remember how to enjoy life. I instructed Linda to let her in when she arrived if I was not home, since I was planning to drive myself to therapy and work the next day.

As I headed up the mound of stairs the phone was ringing again. I thought they got the number changed. No one knew it yet. My heart sped up. After I identified José that morning, I was convinced that he had connections to get my number again. As horrifying as it would be to hear his voice again, my anger was taking over. I'd be damned if I was going to continue to be his victim. I answered.

It was Jerry. He had gotten the new number from Sammy. Dallas must have done the same. He asked if I wanted to go out to dinner. I was hesitant at first (based on me looking like a monster) but I decided to accept.

I went straight for the shower. I needed my long, hot fix to wash off the new filth I had acquired at the jail that morning.

I took a little rest and then got up to attempt the unrealistic task of looking in my closet for something to wear that hid all my wires. I found a loose fitting sundress that had sleeves. The wires were sticking out but it was at least cute.

I wondered if my mother was coming to dinner with us. Though she was not on the top of my good list, she was still my mother. Jerry arrived promptly at eight in his limo. The driver opened the door and I slipped in as gracefully as one could when covered in wires. When Jerry noticed my apparatus he looked a little shocked and tried to make the same joke as Sammy. I was all for lightening our moods and was hoping all this ugly device with its twenty-four hour jolts of pain would soon pay off.

He took me to his "usual Wednesday night hot spot" and told me that my mother was meeting us there later. I didn't mention the problems my mom, Ivan and I were experiencing at that moment deciding to simply enjoy a night out. It had been quite a while since I had been treated and I wasn't going to ruin it by chatting about impossible things.

We pulled up in Jerry's fancy car and all the doormen knew him. A nice looking man escorted us right past the waiting crowd outside and took us straight to our table. Just as we sat down my mother arrived. She kissed Jerry and said a brief hello to me then spent the next twenty minutes talking to Jerry not including me in the conversation. She leaned in toward him and never once looked my way. When she was finished she told Jerry she would see him later, got up and went back to her dancing and socializing. I didn't exactly know what to do. She was flatly rejecting me; acting as though I was invisible. It was incredibly awkward.

Once she was gone, however, Jerry and I had a great time. We talked about how I was going to structure the deal for Joe. I felt extremely grateful to have his mentorship. He gave me the confidence to go in and wow both Sammy and Joe.

It was getting late and signs of exhaustion must have been showing on my frail body because Jerry instructed his driver take me home. I pulled myself up the mountain of stairs and quickly went to bed. Sometime in the middle of the night I was awakened by my own screams. It wasn't the phone - it was just the nightmare of José chasing and cutting me with the knife. Only this time, after the morning's ordeal, his face felt welcome to appear. My heart reacted as though I had been running twenty miles in my sleep. I calmed myself down by thinking of Joe and the prospects of getting Sammy in the black. Like a tranquilizer, those hopes and dreams lulled me back to sleep.

Morning finally came. I was ready to drive myself for the first time. I was nervous as to whether or not I had enough flexibility in my right arm to drive with only one arm. At least I wasn't high on painkillers. First stop: the torture house of therapy, then to my meeting with Joe.

The nice lady at the counter was waiting for me again. After two hours of the same routine, she was amazed with my progress. She knew I had been suffering throughout the aggressive movements, but was pleased to see my progress. She asked how many pills I had taken before I came. I told her I hadn't had one in four days. She was quite surprised by my pain tolerance. I explained how much I hated the way I felt after taking them. She couldn't get over it and said I was one of her most fearless patients. I quickly made my next appointment and said goodbye. I just kept telling myself it was better than the alternative, and that pain was in your head so I blocked it out.

When I got to the hotel there was a message from my mortgage holder about my apartment building. He reminded me that the payment was due the next day. I didn't have it and had no clue what I was going to do. I knew my mother wouldn't pay it. I decided to call him back and explain what happened, hoping maybe he would understand and give me more time. If he didn't, I'd be in the same boat as Sammy - in foreclosure. I dialed the number. This building was so important to me. I rested all my dreams on how great it would be when it was full of happy tenants in such a cute place and how it would be my first real step to being independently wealthy. A woman answered. With my very timid voice, I asked for Mr. Rosen. In a firm voice, she answered, "NO, but may I help you?" I was thinking maybe a woman would be more sympathetic, so I gave it a try and I told her, in my pitiful, disheartened voice, about the terrible thing that had happened to me. I couched it in such a way as not to shock her too much and then said, "So you see - I had a solid plan. It was going great until the man who was already living in the basement went crazy. I'm sure your husband will take that into consideration and give me an extension."

She replied I, "The best I can do is allow you to use the two-week grace period. Otherwise, they will start foreclosure procedures."

I was very familiar with that. I told her I would do my best and said goodbye.

I had to call my mother and let her know the options. I regretfully gave her the bad news. Her answer once again was, "Just sign the property to me and give me all the rent money and I will gladly pay the mortgage." What? She was implying that I was pocketing all the rent money. There wasn't any. She then reminded me she had an appointment with Dan at the end of the week and added "If you lose the building you will still be responsible to pay Ivan all his money back plus interest."

I pleaded with her to come down and see all the improvements in the building. I reminded her that Ivan was very handy and maybe he could come down and help. I really didn't want to give up, especially since I nearly lost my life over it. She just repeated, "Give the property over to me and I'll help Ivan. After all, it was all his money and I need to protect his interest." Then she hung up.

I was a little stunned but not surprised. I began to suspect that Mom invested Ivan's money without his approval.

With a two-week grace period, I was determined to use every last minute of it to make that first mortgage payment. The only problem was I was a little afraid to go to the apartment building by myself. I kept thinking José was going to get out by mistake and come looking for me.

Back at the hotel I spent the rest of the morning on defense for Sammy and working on my presentation to Joe - who was on his way upstairs - so Sammy wouldn't have to go into foreclosure. If Joe was to buy the hotels I might get enough of a commission to pay my building payments and be on my way to my millions.

Joe walked in and immediately focused on my apparatus and wounds. It left him speechless. I told him everything was fine, gave him a brief explanation and a little kiss on the cheek and said, "Let's move on to the properties."

I had a pile of books, records, market research, and other gathered data that I knew would have an impact on him. He told me he was very impressed with my due diligence and that his interest was piqued. We worked

160

together for about five hours. I was both elated and exhausted.

It was clear that we were not going to finish in one day. Deals like these take months, but Sammy didn't have any more time. Joe asked me if I would fly with him to LA to pitch the deal to his partners. He wanted to leave that same night and promised me I would be back in two days. I was excited but I had a few issues. One was the pressure and time limit of the mortgage on my building, but the biggest one was my wonderful probation officer. There was no way he would let me go. I would have to petition the court to get legal permission and that would take months. I became concerned about how to explain to Joe that, though I was pitching a ten million dollar deal, I was actually a jailbird. How exactly was that going to fly?

I took a deep breath, looked squarely in Joe's eyes and said, "Got a minute?"

I told him everything and when I finished he grabbed me, gave me a long, kiss and told me I was still sexy even with all the holes. That was the most thrilling thing to happen to me in years.

He said he would have his plane pick us up in a few hours and he would fly me right back after the meeting. He saw strong potential in the deal, I knew everything about it and he needed me. He also recommended I not tell the probation guy. He promised I would be back before Dan knew I was gone.

I quickly discussed it with Sammy and he told me to go. I wanted to go home and get some things, but Joe said we needed to leave right away and that I could get whatever I needed in LA. Sammy drove us to the airport. Joe's jet was waiting for us to fly in style to LA. With all this excitement - something I hadn't had in a while - I forgot about my electric shocks. That's because sometime between my presentation and confession my battery had died. The sound of the plane's engine lulled me into a deep sleep. I was out for several hours, knowing that we would hit the ground running and I only had a few hours to wow Joe's partners. I was beyond exhausted.

We arrived at LAX and his driver picked us up. First, he took us to Joe's house in Malibu. He lived right on the beach. It was amazing. The sounds of the ocean came right into the living room and the bedroom. It was so peaceful.

Next, Joe ordered his driver to take me shopping to get something to wear for the meeting and replace my batteries. I didn't have very much money and was hoping there was a dollar store somewhere in Beverly Hills. Instead, the driver took me straight to Rodeo Drive where we pulled up to a famous, expensive couture store. I looked at the driver and sheepishly told him I didn't bring my wallet - hoping he didn't want to go back to get it. He told me not to worry about a thing because he had Joe's credit card and that he takes all Joe's girls shopping. I hated that comment I felt like an Ike girl for a moment.

The driver commanded me to get out of the car and get something awesome for the meeting in the morning. I went straight to the sale rack, looking at outfits starting at the five hundred dollar range - one quarter of my mortgage payment. I used to shop like that all the time, but only when I had the money. When the saleslady came over to assist me she took one look and took off. I guess I looked like a beat up prostitute. I helped myself to a nice looking dress and some beautiful underwear, the driver paid with Joe's AMEX and we headed over to the hardware store for batteries.

Arriving back at his house, I noticed his Ferrari was not in the driveway. The driver let me in and I found a note that said he had a meeting and would be back later.

He told me to get some sleep so I would be ready for the next day. The driver left and I made myself at home. The peaceful sounds of the Pacific Ocean gave me the rare opportunity to tune out my busy thoughts and I passed out before I could sabotage nature's gift.

Sometime in the middle of the night I thought I heard someone. I woke up to my own screaming. "Stop! Please stop!" Joe rushed in and I started hitting and fighting him. I was confused. Joe snapped me into reality and told me I was just having a bad dream. He stroked my hair until I fell back to sleep.

The next morning I woke up early, ready for my second presentation. Joe's partner was coming at ten. That gave me plenty of time to disconnect myself from my wires and take a hot shower. I even took advantage of the fresh ocean air and went for a brief walk to focus on my deal.

When his partner arrived I was totally ready. I began by telling him how much he wanted to be in the hotel business in Miami Beach. I explained all the advantages, the trends, went over the profits and losses and made him aware of all the comps of neighboring hotels.

I got some promising responses. He was very brief, though. He got up and told Joe he would be in touch. That was it? I came all the way for that? I discussed it with Joe and his response was that my meeting lasted longer than usual, which he considered to be a good sign.

Joe took me to lunch and back to his plane before I got caught by the evil Dan. Joe didn't join me on the flight. He told me he would crunch the numbers and see if the hotels fit in his portfolio. He then gave me one of those great kisses and told me to take care of myself. My response was, I do.

Sammy was waiting at the Miami Airport to pick me up, anxiously awaiting the details. I kept the part about the meeting only lasting twenty minutes to myself; I just told him it went well. We both kept our fingers crossed.

I wanted to stop at the building on the way to the hotel. Sammy only had a few minutes and I could see he was a little squirmy about going to the scene of the crime. As we drove up I noticed the fresh paint on the outside. It looked quite cute, but it didn't erase the pain and ugliness that went on behind closed doors just a month before.

I slowly walked inside and realized how creepy it was. I wondered if prospective tenants were feeling the same thing. Old Neighbor Lady came out of Apartment Five. She quickly brought me up to speed. She had three new tenants move in, but they wanted the same deal - to fix up the older ones and not pay rent. She had accepted their offer. Though it was good to have three more apartments ready, it still didn't take of the looming mortgage problem. I reminded her that we needed *paying* customers right now. I didn't want to scare her about the potential foreclosure. Sammy was outside, impatiently blowing the horn and alerting me that it was time to go. I scooted out the door wishing Old Neighbor Lady good luck and thanked her for her efforts.

Back at the hotel a message from Mr. Rosen, the lender, was waiting for me. I called him back, planning on killing him with enthusiasm. Maybe he would see the upside and give me another month. I cannot say why this particular building, especially with its recent bad history, was still all-important to me, but it was. I was not the kind of person who caved when the hard parts reared up. My determination was running the show now. I was not a quitter.

Although he said he was sorry to hear what happened to me and he was glad to know I was okay, he gave me the same answer his wife did. If I couldn't pay him next week he advised signing the building back to him to avoid costly foreclosures and bad credit I would just lose my (AND my brother's) down payment. I replied that I would have to think about it. I still had eight more days and was not about to give up. I finished up some paperwork for Sammy and headed home exhausted.

Dallas was waiting at my place. She didn't look so beautiful, but who was I to talk? At least she wasn't full of wires and holes. She hugged me and told me how sorry she was that I got so messed up. She asked if she could stay with me for a little while. She said New York was getting out of control and she needed me to keep her in line. That's just what I needed; another person to add to my list of responsibilities.

Jerry called and wanted to take me out to Fisher Island to hear about my escapade in Los Angeles. I told him Dallas was visiting. He had met her before and invited her to come along. I never asked, but somehow I knew my mother and Jerry weren't ever seeing each other exclusively so I wasn't worried about Dallas' eagerness to connect with him. She went for rich men - big, fat, ugly, short, tall, handsome or gross - as long as they had plenty of money she would be on full flirt tilt.

I took my overdue, hot shower. I needed to let the tension of the long flight, Mr. Rosen's pressure, the million-dollar deal and the bad vibes from the building go down the drain with the gentle flow of water. Then I got a good hour's worth of rest in before preparing for a night out.

The driver picked us up promptly at eight. I gracefully got in the car - wires and all. Dallas made sure to sit right next to Jerry who looked carefully at my wounds to see if I was healing properly. He was genuinely concerned. Dallas put on her best charm. Here we go again: I had the brains - she had the sex appeal. I could tell Jerry was not interested in intelligence this night.

We arrived at the ferry in Miami that takes exclusive members to a private island. We had dinner at the swanky place and I caught him up about the deal.

The thing I loved most about Jerry was that he always acted like he was proud of me. He constantly introduced me as his daughter. That was the greatest title I could have with such a kind and powerful man. God, I wished it were true but I enjoyed my fantasy anyway. He didn't have kids and I didn't have a dad, so it was perfect.

Dallas was in full flirt throttle and I was fading quickly. Exhaustion was taking over. I did not have the luxury of being inactive until I was completely healed. Nor was it in my nature to lay around feeling sorry for myself. But when I would get fatigued I'd go into pain mode; I needed to go home.

Jerry instructed the driver to take me back alone then come for him and Dallas later. Having fallen sound asleep in the limo, the driver woke me up and walked me up stairs and politely said good night.

As tired as I was, the throbbing pain in my reattached finger was robbing me of slumber. Instead, I obsessed about my appointment with Dan the probation man knowing he had met with my mother the previous day.

Just as I talked myself into sleep I heard Dallas coming in. It must have been four a.m. Some things never change. I didn't want to know what happened.

As soon as morning came I got dressed, reconnected my wires, put my pitiful face on and headed down to probation.

Arriving at his smelly office, there were five other convicts, all male, waiting outside in line for the bathroom holding plastic cups. After I took my turn I had to remain there for two and a half hours holding my warm urine in my hand, making sure no one switched with me; one of the tricks I learned in jail.

Dan harshly closed the door behind me. It was nerve-wracking to know that this man, who hated me, maintained so much control over my life.

With a smirk on his face he got right to the point. "I visited with your mother yesterday. Interesting woman."

I wasn't sure if that was a good thing or a bad thing.

"She told me she was worried about the building and that maybe you shouldn't own it anymore. She told me that you couldn't afford it and that after what happened it might be too dangerous," he reported. Without letting me explain a thing, he proclaimed, "You need to consider getting rid of it."

I gave him a blank stare.

"You also need to start your community service, which will occupy most of your time." He followed that by handing me a list of acceptable community service jobs I could choose from. I told him I would make a decision and get back to him.

On my way out of the door I heard him mutter, "Your urine is clean."

No time to stop at the building as I needed to get to work to find out if there were any messages from Joe about buying the hotel. I marched into the lobby and looked through a whole stack. Most were from Sammy's bill collectors, followed by a message from Jerry and the one from Joe. It said to call him ASAP.

All I could think about was putting this deal together. I was so nervous I could not dial the number. After the third time it started to ring. Joe answered. First, he asked how I was doing and how nice it was to see me - and more of all the nice things people who are polite ask. I'm afraid I wasn't as courteous, as I answered with short, monosyllabic words. I was dying to get to the good parts. He then said the deal didn't fit in his portfolio, but he sold it to a different partnership and they wanted to close quickly! They were not going to pay the full asking price but it was a fair deal. I then put him in touch with Sammy's bankruptcy lawyer. Again, I think my manners left me because I quickly got off and ran downstairs to tell Sammy the news.

Wait a minute - I realized I might have sold myself out of a job. What was I going to do now? It didn't sound like there would be any money left for my building or me.

I gave Sammy the news. He had already heard from his lawyer and they were working on it. I hobbled back upstairs to call Jerry. In a small way I was excited to be a part of this deal, but sad it was almost over.

Jerry was more excited than me. He told me it was perfect timing because he had a new job for me and he needed me right away. I immediately got energized again.

I had an appointment later that day with my doctor to take the stitches out. When I walked in his office he was amazed to see I was the same person. He glowed as he told me I was healing nicely. I was pleased I had followed his instructions and used the cream every day to help lighten the scaring. He then told me I still had a long way to go with my arm and finger, but I should gain back most use as long as I wore the wire contraption and continued with therapy. With the weight of the two hundred stitches gone, I made my next appointment and swiftly got out of there.

I couldn't wait to call Jerry to make sure he was serious about a job. Dallas met me at the door and wanted to know where we were partying that night. I moved her out of the way and ran to the phone to call him. He answered on the first ring as if he was waiting for my call. He told me he had bought a piece of real estate nearby in Hollywood that had some RV's on it. He wanted me to get rid of them so he could develop the property. I didn't know what that meant, but I was eager to find out.

I told Dallas I wanted to get a good night sleep because I had a lot to do the next day. She understood and promptly replaced me with some other partygoers.

I took my usual hot, cleansing shower that ran smoothly over my stitch-free, diminishing scars, crawled into bed and thought about what an interesting day it had been.

The morning came and I was so excited it seemed to take forever to drive to the hotel to make sure the deal was still going okay and there were no new problems to prevent the closing. With only two days left on my grace period for my mortgage payments, I thought I would call Mr. Rosen one more time and see if he found some compassion.

I went upstairs to my office to call him in private. I didn't want anyone to hear me grovel. It turned out he was waiting for my call and the first words out of his mouth were, "Do you have my money?"

It didn't sound like compassion to me. Mr. Rosen offered to take the property back with no further obligation. All I would lose was my (Ivan's) down payment. He promised it would not affect my credit and we wouldn't get involved in a costly foreclosure.

I asked him if I could call him back in a few minutes and went back downstairs to talk to Sammy. I was good at fixing up Sammy's problems and giving him sound advice; it was time he gave me some. He agreed with Mr. Rosen and thought it was in my best interest to walk away. I argued the fact that I was not a quitter, I never give up. Sammy advised that in this case I needed to quit - and that the building had a curse. He encouraged me to spend my energy on a winning project.

He did have a point.

I then called Jerry to garner his opinion. He answered the phone right away. He encouraged me not to think of myself as a loser and that as soon as I put my mind to it I would be a winner and twice as big - in something else. At that moment I knew I had to move on.

I called Mr. Rosen and asked him what paperwork I needed to sign, as I was giving the building back to him. It was killing me to do this, even though the building almost killed me. He set up an appointment at his lawyer's office.

My next call was to Barry, the intern. He was the only person in my price range who could check the paperwork before I signed it.

I was afraid to call my mother, but I had to. I dialed and it rang many times. As I was just about to hang up, she answered. I told her what I was going to do. She didn't care, but said I still needed to pay Ivan back. I didn't understand that; I lost my money all my hard work, and almost my life. What kind of guarantee was *I* getting? It didn't matter. I was doomed to pay him back some day. At that moment I didn't have two nickels to rub together, so I told her I would sign an IOU. She said fine and that she would write something up and I could sign it and do whatever I wanted with the building. I didn't really understand that I seemed to be the only one to lose everything but arguing with her wasn't going anywhere.

It was only noon and I felt like the whole world just fell on me. What else would be in store for the second half of the day?

I had a few details to finish at the hotel then I wanted to call Jerry about the job.

Chapter 21
LITTLE HOUSES ON WHEELS

Jerry and I were meeting at the property to check out my new job right after work, and Sammy and I made plans to meet at Turnberry later to celebrate the sale of his hotel. I was determined to turn the day into something positive.

Driving as fast as I could with wires still in tow, I arrived at the property. There were a bunch of cute little houses on wheels; I guessed those must be the RVs he was talking about. Clueless, I had to research that RV stood for recreational vehicle.

Jerry was inside talking with an older, large man. They seemed to be arguing, but I didn't want to be nosy. There was also a young French Canadian boy standing outside. He seemed nice. He noticed my scars and seemed genuinely concerned - a rare reaction. We started talking about the company.

Jerry came out of the office with Bob, the old man, and introduced me as his daughter. He then added that I was going to work there as a salesman.

I could tell by the look on Bob's face that this little piece of news, which was also news to me, was not making him happy. As soon as Jerry went to use the restroom, Bob was quick to tell me with quite a gruff attitude that they were closing right then and would reopen at ten the next morning. He let me know that there was not much for me to do; that he and Stephan could cover things but if I wanted to waste Jerry's money I could come back at ten the next day.

As soon as Jerry came back Bob changed his tone, put on a big, fake smile and told me he was looking forward to working with me and pushed us both out the door.

Jerry instructed me to be there bright and early. The priority was to get rid of those cute houses on wheels. He bought the property and was about $350,000 in the hole until they were liquidated. Good old Bob had not sold any in about three weeks. Jerry knew I could sell ice to an Eskimo.

I enthusiastically told him I would be there in the morning - no problem.

Rushing home I went to work on my social life. I was to meet Sammy and Dallas at Turnberry.

Dallas was waiting at the door of my house with a note in her hand. I was afraid to read it at first. It was from Linda. She explained that she was moving out of state since it seemed that I was healed enough to take care of myself and that she would be in touch and good bye. I thought that was a little cold, but oh well.

I was excited to tell Dallas about my new job and the cute little houses. She responded with, "What time are we going to Turnberry" and, "whose meeting us?" For a moment there I forgot whom I was talking to. I told her I needed a nap and then I would get ready. Sammy was meeting us at ten p.m.

Between the time I spent living in New York, in jail, and in the hospital, I felt out of touch with my party pals. I was all set to get back to some playtime. My only hesitation was that no one had seen Scarface yet. I once again reminded myself that it was better than having my friends standing over my graveside.

I decided to forgo the torture contraption for a night and donned a real party dress. I chose a color that complimented my fresh pink scars and swollen limbs.

As soon Dallas, Sammy and I sat down in our usual VIP section, Sammy's girls began to flock like little pigeons to an old man's crumbs, cooing and adjusting themselves to get the best pieces of bread. In this case it was champagne. My friends Linda, Lisa, Donna and

Lynn had heard about the accident and were eager to put a smile back on my face and start dancing. I finally felt like my old self again.

Dallas started working the crowd. She knew if she found just the right gentleman, he would lead her to the golden drug of choice. She began, as always, with the owner, Don. He responded by sending us over a few bottles of the bubbly and told us to join him on the Monkey Business yacht for a private party. Bulls eye - exactly what Dallas was aiming for.

I had a little champagne and danced a bit. I had not had any alcohol in so long I was getting drunk on my first glass, so I thought I would cool it. I was wound up about starting my new job the next day. Though the evening was a perfect way to release and provided a chance to feel normal again, my priority was to show Jerry my chops.

Sometime around two, I was getting quite tired and went looking for Dallas to see if she was going home with me. Though it was rarely the case, I always gave her the courtesy of asking. George The doorman told me she was on The Monkey Business. It was always cool to go on the boat. All celebrities who happened to be in town would hang there. You had to be invited and you had to pass Don's inspection in the looks department to get on the boat. Though I had partied there many times, it was really a scene set up for overt sex and drugs and rich men, which was not my style. However, I did love to hook up with Tony as he was one of the few people that understood me. It didn't hurt that he was sexy, either. He and I got along very well, especially because there were no strings attached. As soon as I entered the boat he saw me. I had missed this part of my life, so when I caught his eye I gave a big smile. His face said it all. My less-than-perfect condition trying to pass for "pretty in a party dress" did not get past him. He said hello and walked right past my scar tissue.

I didn't see Dallas anywhere, and then an inebriated woman told me she was down below. Unless I wanted to head for wild sex and mounds of cocaine, I knew better than going below deck. It was a dimly lit place with pulsating techno music and orgy-like visions of throbbing bodies in constant slow motion. Dallas was also into girls. I always knew that, but thank god she never came on to me. I decided to go home before I got dragged downstairs.

Going back through the club I saw Sammy with three girls fussing over him. He was so cute all the girls loved him. I said good-bye and drove myself home.

After reattaching my left side to its electrical harness, I had only a few hours of sleep to catch before I started my new adventure in Recreational Vehicle Land. Even though it was a temporary job, the way I handled it could dictate my future with Jerry. The sooner I got rid of the little houses on wheels, the more impressed he'd be. And maybe I could have a hand in either developing that land or helping him sell it for a profit. I drifted off picturing myself making those millions of dollars that had been waiting for me. I was back on track.

Morning came and I covered my wires with casual business clothes and headed out to the property a little early. I liked to be "more than ready" for any new journey. I sat outside the locked door chatting with my new friend Stephan, the young French Canadian salesman. He was tall and cute with a lean, athletic body and pretty green eyes. His sexy French accent was a nice bonus. He was twenty and I was twenty-four with a lot of road behind me. We both waited outside for Bob.

Several customers began to arrive with intentions of finding out the details about buying the RVs. We didn't have any keys, so we kept them entertained as best we

174

could so they wouldn't get frustrated and leave. Bob finally arrived at ten-thirty. He took one look at me and scowled. I immediately brought his attention to the potential customers. He pushed me aside and started directing Stephan around like I was not there.

Within the first two hours I notice at least a dozen unhappy customers coming and going. Since they were all French Canadian and spoke to Stephan in their language I could only tell from the tone of their conversations and body language that they were not at all pleased with the information.

I was eager to help. When I tried to find out from Bob what was going on, he told me that those people were too demanding. He said they wanted everything free and were very picky about the quality. He said I was to ignore them and let Stephan do what he had to. I was supposed to concentrate on the new ones. I think he was planning to tell Jerry what a waste of time and his money I was.

I decided to follow Stephan around to find out as much as I could. I was eager to learn about the houses we were selling, how they were made, the quality of the construction, warrantees, options available and color choices.

Bob was ready to close shop at four in the afternoon and there were plenty of customers milling around the models with interest. He didn't care. He repeated that the hours were ten to four with no exceptions. He told them to come back the next day. I was confused about Bob's intentions. It didn't seem like he cared about selling the RVs, Jerry's money or business. But this was just my first day. I'd give him the benefit of the doubt - for now.

When I got home it looked as though Dallas had just walked in the door, too. She was a mess from hearty partying all night. She said she was leaving for New York the next day and would stay for about a week or so. She said was running out of money so she would be back to help me with some rent money. In the same breath she wanted to know what we were doing later that night. She was beginning to exhaust me. I told her I needed a nap and maybe we would go to the Cricket Club.

Thanksgiving was coming in two days and I was wondering what I was going to do. I didn't want to cook dinner by myself. Since Dallas was leaving, I thought I would call Jerry and tell him about the day with Bob and invite him for Thanksgiving. I also planned on calling Barry, the intern, and Sammy.

Jerry was delighted to hear from me. In keeping with my "wait and see" attitude about Bob, I didn't have much news to report about work. He was happy about the Thanksgiving invite, but asked if I had planned on having my mother join us. That was an odd question, as I would have preferred to be thankful with people who were a positive part of my life and my mother did not qualify. I was a little confused about why he had asked that. He clarified by telling me he no longer wanted anything to do with her and he would not come over if she were there. When I asked why, he said that ever since the night we went to the restaurant when I was still so injured and had just gotten my wires attached and was obviously in pain, he was shocked and disgusted that my mother didn't even ask what they were and how I was feeling. Her blatant callousness put him off. I hadn't noticed anything different because I was so used to it, it didn't bother me. But there was a small part of me that did a tiny, unnoticeable happy dance that Jerry was sticking up for me.

Barry said he would come over, but Sammy could not, as he was seeing his kids. Barry was excited to have dinner with such a powerful man as Jerry. Now that my Thanksgiving plans were organized, I took my long, hot shower and washed away the unhappy customers. Then I took my nap so I could be ready for Dallas and the Cricket Club.

After Tony's rejection at Turnberry, I stressed a little over what dress would correctly cover my ugly imperfections. I decided to forgo the wires again and wear something with sleeves that concealed my freshly scarred flesh. I was transitioning back into the life I enjoyed before jail and the assault and wanted to steer clear of any negative attention.

In the cutest outfit I could come up with, Dallas and I headed for the Cricket Club to meet Sammy, Donna and Lynn. I figured I would probably run into the owner's son, Mark, the hottie I flirted with before going to the hole. But would he snub me like Tony?

Arriving at the club was like going to the Oscars; hundreds of people outside its private exterior trying to get in, hoping to find their names on the exclusive guest list. The crowd was moved to the side for Dallas and me to pass. We were quickly guided to the VIP section where a bottle of Dom was waiting. I wasn't sure whom Dallas was courting that night - but I was happy to participate in the drinking.

My garment choice must have worked because no one in the packed house gawked at me. Most of my friends were aware of what had happened to me and were delighted to see I was there no matter what I looked like. They made me feel better.

When I saw Mark standing across the room, I started reminiscing about the last time I was with him. It was amazing. I hesitated, not sure if I was ready to expose my less-than-perfect self, but as soon as he saw me he came right over. He instantly noticed my condition and hugged me as I explained about my tragic ordeal. We talked for a while, and just as I was thinking we were going to hook up again, he told me he was getting married. I was starting to think I put men in the marrying mood; that is, the mood to marry someone else. He did not let go of my hand and continued to look me in the eyes as he told me about his arranged marriage with the princess of Saudi Arabia. After a few more hours of mingling I needed to go to sleep. I wanted to be well rested to tackle Bob and all the unhappy customers. I quietly snuck out so Donna and Lynn didn't try to talk me into staying later. Dallas was MIA.

Waking bright and early, I could not wait to get to the job. Worrisome white smoke started bellowing out from the hood of my car as I drove slowly through traffic. I was only a few miles away so I elected to keep going. I pulled into the lot with deep white smoke following me. Stephan was there to rescue me. I had noticed my watch - it was only ten minutes after nine. Bob doesn't get there till ten or later so I asked Stephan if he happened to have a key. No such luck.

Stephan popped open the hood and saw I had a broken hose. He assured me that he would fix it right away. I was enjoying the idea that he was so eager to come to my rescue.

Bob finally arrived a little after ten. It was a rather quiet day as far as customers were concerned. They were probably out shopping for Thanksgiving fixings the next day. Bob mentioned that we would be closing early for family day. By the time I sorted out my plans for the day, Bob announced we were closing in thirty minutes.

I said my good-bye to Stephan and wished him Happy Thanksgiving, then called Jerry to confirm the plans for our holiday dinner. He asked me once more if I had invited my mother. I told him I had not heard from her, so I was assuming she was not interested. Relieved, he kindly volunteered to pick up the turkey and have his driver drop it off at my house.

As I drove off the lot I started wondering about Stephan and why he was always there so early. Thinking maybe he was here without any family, I slightly regretted not inviting him for Thanksgiving.

I stopped by the store with all the other Floridians who were gathering the fixings for the holiday. I was excited. I had never cooked a turkey or hosted this kind of special event and now I was preparing to spend a whole evening with a powerful man who was overloaded with wisdom. I planned to spend my whole dinner extracting knowledge out of Jerry's and Barry's heads and installing it into mine.

As I tried to negotiate all the groceries into my place, the phone was pressing me to answer. I was hoping no one was canceling. It was my mother probing about what my plans were. She didn't necessarily want to see me; she was searching for Jerry answers. She complained that he was no longer taking her calls. I gave a little involuntary smile and then admonished myself. She wanted to know if I knew why he didn't. The temptation was to respond, "Mother, Jerry told me that he was so thoroughly disgusted with the way you treated me and he wants nothing more to do with you. So, you can no longer sponge off of him. Too bad for you." After three times changing the subject, I finally admitted I was cooking dinner for Jerry and Barry and added, "I didn't know you were interested in joining us. I'm really sorry, but I only have a little food." If I had been open to having her join us I would have also opened myself up to her utter domination. Jerry would have refused to come and she would have backed out because of him. No, I could not ask her even though she continued to be very persistence about inviting herself. I told her we had a business meeting with Barry. She said fine and begged me to find out why Jerry was mad at her; I told her I would find out if I could and wished her Happy Thanksgiving. I quickly got off the phone to tend to my recipe.

With Linda gone, Dallas off to NY and Sammy spending the next few days with his kids, I was going to be home alone that night for the first time. I was tired and couldn't wait to take my long, sedating, hot shower and wash away my not-so-bad day. I crawled into bed with wires sparking my nerves and healing my arm. I fell asleep thinking of the other ways I'd been healing, as well. I stood up to my mother in my own way, I had a new, challenging job with new hope, I was actually entertaining two fascinating men the next day, I was stitch-free and I was alive!

Sometime in the middle of the night I heard a woman screaming. It was me, of course. I couldn't shake the sensation that José was in the room watching over me. Once again I had to tell myself that it was just a bad dream. I got up and went into my favorite place - the shower. I stood under the comforting hot water, letting it rinse away the terrible grip my attacker still had on me. About a half an hour later it finally worked.

I woke up tired; as if I had run a marathon all night. Yet I was energized by the anticipation of my new cooking job. I got downstairs as fast as I could so I could remove the turkey from the refrigerator, but I couldn't lift it with my worthless left arm. What would I do if it couldn't get in the oven? I decided to go next door to the neighbor and ask him for help. I was not very good at this, but I had to do it. The neighbor man was happy to lend a hand and volunteered to come back to take it out of the oven and place it on the table. It was perfect. I would still be able to impress Jerry and Barry with my domestic qualities while I was implanting their moneymaking brains into mine.

I spent the rest of the morning and a good part of the afternoon creating all the wonderful side dishes that go with a traditional Thanksgiving dinner. When I commit to something, I do it full on. This was going to be an amazing meal. Jerry entered the house and was overly impressed with the aroma coming from the kitchen. I then had to break it to him that I needed to get help from the neighbor man. Jerry thought that was funny and I still carried out my plan. Barry showed up a little later. We were one peculiar, but happy, family on this night of thanks.

Jerry mesmerized Barry and me for over two hours with deals he did and amounts of money he made. He then pulled out an envelope with two thousand, five hundred dollars in it and ceremoniously handed it to me. He said that represented the commission I earned on the profits he made doing the mortgage of Sammy's hotel. I was so happy. It had been a long time since I had made money. Jerry and I had never discussed how much I was to be paid for selling the little houses but on this magical night I had an envelope full.

After a fulfilling evening of stimulating business chat, the men excused themselves and I spent the next few hours cleaning up. I topped the night off with my favorite new addiction - the hot shower. I couldn't have asked for a better holiday.

Up early and ready for work; the only problem was it was only eight. I couldn't stand the fact that work didn't start until ten. I thought I would go anyway and see if Stephan was there. Driving slowly through traffic, my car started giving me trouble again. I drifted into the lot and there was Stephan sitting outside with a big grin on his face. I asked him why he was there so early and he told me he was living in a trailer in the back. He had come to Florida to race motorcycles and needed this job to pay for his racing. That was not the answer I was expecting, but it sounded exciting.

Bob finally arrived and so did the unhappy customers. This time I was going to find out why. They came in yelling that Bob had promised he was going to be at their place to fix the little house they bought a few weeks back. Bob told Stephan to go see them later that day. This did not make any sense, so I stepped up and insisted that Bob send him right then. I added that I would go with him to help. Bob was not happy with my demands and told Stephan to stay right there and then he told the customer that Stephan would be there soon.

"Little Lady, you've got a lot to learn," he said with disdain. "Shouldn't you be home makin' babies or somethin'?" He puffed up a bit at his own gall.

Dan, the Probation Man, carrying the little pee cup interrupted my clever comeback. Jesus Christ. Why does he have to make sure everyone and their brothers know I have a probation officer? What was he doing? I already notified him about my new employment and was scheduled to see him the following week. He had it out for me.

He made sure to walk by Bob holding the cup in plain sight, looking for his sample. Why wouldn't he be discreet? Wouldn't you think the goal here would be to make sure his ward could fit back into society and make a new, worthwhile life? I hoped he didn't talk with Bob. Good ole Bob would jump at the chance to get rid of me.

I took the cup quickly, trying to hide it as I made my way to the bathroom. I convinced Dan that Bob was not my boss, and that Jerry was, and let him know that Jerry was familiar with my situation, so it wouldn't be a problem. Dan took my warm urine with him and said, "Good bye." He paused to catch my glance and added with a sinister smile, "It better be clean."

"Who was that?" Bob had watched the whole thing like a hawk.

"Oh, he's just a guy. It's nothing." It was none of his business.

"Listen to me, little lady. This is a legitimate company. If you are doing anything illegal I will make damn sure you will not see daylight for a long time." He seemed eager to make good on the threat.

One of the many drawbacks of being on probation was that you are stripped of any privacy. I had to confess but all Bob heard was a great rationale to get rid of me.

"I don't like this one bit. This business is licensed by the State of Florida and no criminals are allowed to work here, so you better start looking for employment elsewhere," he righteously informed me. "And don't think I won't call Jerry with this information."

"Jerry knows everything. I'm not going anywhere," I countered.

Just then I looked out the door and saw two customers I had spoken to a few days back. I excused myself so Bob could go tattle on me while I addressed a potential sale. I approached them with enthusiasm. The Canadian man wanted to know what my best price was on the blue house.

Excited, I went back to Bob to find out what the best price would be. I figured he would put our differences aside for one minute so he could close this deal. Bob didn't negotiate much. I had to explain that Jerry just wanted to get rid of them. We went back and forth for about twenty minutes. I was getting nervous that the couple would take off. Finally, Bob came down on the price.

I went back to the Canadian couple and told the husband that the only way I could come down on the price is if he brought me three new customers. I upped the ante by offering them a commission on any sales that went through with their referrals. He was very pleased with this offer, so I brought him into the office.

The hardest part of these kinds of sales is getting the customer to actually let go of his money. He said he didn't have much faith in our service, so he would give one thousand dollars as a deposit and promised to pay the balance when the house was installed to his satisfaction.

I knew if I was in charge he would be satisfied on the first day, but that was not the case. I had to rely on Bob and his empty promises. I hoped the fact that Bob was still owed money would be incentive for him to work harder to get the balance. Stephan and I made plans to deliver the house the next day. It was my first sale so I needed it to be perfect.

I was bursting with excitement and rushed past Bob to use the phone to let Jerry know the good news. He answered quickly, as if he was expecting to hear from me. Before I could tell him about my first sale, he told me in a quiet and subdued voice that he had gotten a call from Bob. My heart sank. He went on to say he needed to talk with me and to meet him for dinner at eight. I agreed but all my enthusiasm went out the window. What if Jerry was influenced by Bob and decided this wouldn't work out?

I never even told him about the sale.

Bob started yelling that it was four o'clock and it was time to close. I wanted to stay a little longer to make sure everything was organized and there was nothing wrong with my little blue house. No such luck. Bob practically pushed me out the door, turned the open sign around and locked the door. I tried to ask him if I could come early to inspect the house before delivery, but he walked by me like I wasn't there.

I said my good bye to Stephan and drove off in my not-so-perfect car. I went back to my empty house and headed straight for the shower. I needed the pure water to wash Dan and Bob's negativity off.

The nap was useless. I just stared at the ceiling worrying about my future. I was highly frustrated. I knew I could sell the hell out of those little houses on wheels and yet I had two aggressive bulls in the ring with me - razor-sharp horns ready to toss me out if I so much as moved a finger.

Lingering in my challenging closet I searched for something cute but professional. I wanted Jerry to think I was almost healed so he wouldn't consider me handicapped in any way. I elected to leave the wires on my dresser.

I arrived at the Jockey Club fifteen minutes early. The Maître d' walked me back to the table where Jerry was sitting.

The minute I sat down I blurted out that I made a sale; - just in case he didn't have beneficial plans for me. He shared in my excitement and wanted details. When he asked me what was going on with Bob, I wasn't sure how to answer. I didn't know how friendly they were. I didn't want to rat on him and have it backfire on me. I did let on about the unhappy customers and my plan about offering them a commission if they brought in three more buying customers. He wanted to know why they were unhappy. I told him Bob made promises he didn't keep. In the next breath he said that they were going to be my problem from now on and that I had better figure out what I was going to do to make them happy. I was confused. He then said he was firing Bob the next morning. He added that he hoped I had learned something in the week I was there.

I was dumbfounded. I thought I was fighting for my life to keep this job. I had no idea that's where Jerry's conversation was headed. Poor Bob. Now I felt bad for him.

I was hoping Jerry was planning to do the firing because if it were to be my new duty, Bob would probably finish where José left off. Thank god Jerry said he would be there by nine to take care of it. I had to tell him Bob didn't get there till ten. He was not happy about that. I proudly informed him that under my rule, we would be open at nine a.m. till at least six p.m. because I noticed a lot of customers came at the end of the day.

Thrilled about my new position I quickly ate up my delicious dinner and excused myself to go home and make my plans.

Morning couldn't come early enough. I rushed to get ready and ran out the door with the enthusiasm of a child headed for Disney World. Then I remembered I didn't want to be there when Bob got fired. My curiosity got the better of me when I pulled into the lot to see Bob getting blasted in the office by Jerry. I was a little afraid for Jerry, thinking maybe Bob would hurt him. Jerry was much older and smaller than Bob. I busted in the door and Bob turned his anger on me. He glared at Jerry and said, "You are willing to believe this jailbird crook over me?"

"Yes," Jerry said as clearly as possible.

Bob then grabbed his personal things and kicked the door open with his foot.

I didn't really know much about the little houses, but I guessed I was about to learn quickly. Stephan slowly came in from his parked trailer in the back. Jerry and I filled him in on what had happened. Jerry then introduced me as the new manager. Stephan reminded me about our delivery. We said goodbye as Jerry drove off to his big fancy office in Bal Harbor.

On his way out, he passed the deliveryman who was hired to tow the little blue house to its new owners. Stephan and I jumped in his little truck with a milk crate full of tools. Stephan had delivered a few of these before and I knew I would be able to rely on my experience from my construction company days to figure this out.

There were about one hundred people outside the site waiting for the arrival of the new house. All I could see were potential customers. I told Stephan we had to make this one perfect. He understood completely.

We took our jobs seriously as we leveled the house, removed the wheels, set up the furniture and hooked up the plumbing. I had to go back and forth from the park to our office to get parts and check on things. I was concerned because I left it closed with a sign on the door "BACK SOON".

In between settling the blue house I mingled with the crowd to see how many could become my new customers. My enthusiasm was contagious and many said they were eager to come by the lot, but wanted to stay and see the finished product.

With my part of the delivery complete, I went back to the office and waited for Stephan. Over the next two hours, several more Canadians came to visit the little houses like the one that had just got delivered to their park.

Stephan came back a little after six, dirty and exhausted. I was so happy with all his efforts I offered to take him for some dinner. He released a big grin and quickly accepted my invitation. It was nothing fancy - just the cute little Italian restaurant next door. I do believe Stephan was thoroughly impressed because he began to look at me with big ole puppy dog eyes. He was cute, but too young for me. I gave him a few small eye contacts back, paid for dinner and left. Stephan couldn't thank me enough.

When I got home I could not wait to call Jerry and tell him how great everything had been. He shared my enthusiasm and instructed me to call him as soon as I got the rest of the money. I said goodbye and couldn't wait to get into the shower. This time I had actual dirt to wash off from crawling under the little blue house. I languished under the hot water absorbing a great feeling of accomplishment. This was the first time I didn't have to use it to help me escape an intolerable reality.

Sammy called and wanted me to meet him at Turnberry. I checked my messages to hear Donna and Lynn extending an invitation as well. I felt like a whole new person. As I lay down, I basked in gratitude for getting the chance for a fresh start.

Turnberry was packed. I headed over to Sammy's usual spot. He gave me a little peck on the cheek and complimented me on how good I looked. My friend Lynn signaled me over. She wanted me to party with her and Donna on the Monkey Business. She said there were very important guests on the boat tonight. I was intrigued, so I gathered my bag and told Sammy I'd see him later.

The three of us got to the dock and noticed a lot of bodyguards outside. Lynn grabbed me and Donna's hand, pushed through the crowd and guided us onto the boat. Don was waiting for us; he liked his pretty girls to decorate the Monkey Business.

The boat was a little darker than usual. I noticed a handsome man who looked very familiar. The waiter came over to us with champagne. The handsome man held up his glass in a mock toast and we walked right over to accommodate. We were in full flirt mode when Don came over and introduced us.

"Girls, I'd like you to meet Gary."

"Gary, this is Gigi, Donna and Lynn. They're here to have a little fun, right girls?"

We giggled appropriately and continued our flirting. I hadn't felt this good since I was younger and much more innocent. I had experienced a fantastic day and the champagne tasted especially good that night in my sexy dress without wires.

I could not place where I had met Gary, but it didn't matter; we drank two more bottles and were getting silly. Gary was really funny, so the entertainment was mutual. Lynn had her camera with her and she started taking pictures. Donna was hamming it up sitting on Gary's lap.

Then Lynn and I took our turns on his lap for a photo. He was all over us. Playful hands were groping both of us. I wasn't as comfortable as Donna. I didn't want him to come across any scar tissue. I didn't notice his wedding ring, but it wasn't unusual for married men to party there.

It was bothering me as to where I might have met him before, so I finally asked.

Donna was still on his lap. I think he liked her.

He leaned in close to me and said in a very quiet voice, "I'm Gary Hart."

Donna leaned in and added, "He's running for President of the United States!"

I couldn't believe that a powerful man like that would be at a party like this. He was married and high profile. I wasn't so sure being on the boat with him was such a good thing but Donna and Lynn didn't seem to care. All I could think of was that somehow I would get accused of something illegal and I'd end up back in jail. I excused myself by saying I was going to the bathroom, got off the boat and went back upstairs. I didn't see Sammy so I drove myself home and crawled into bed to focus on what had just happened.

I woke up way before the alarm again the next morning with the energy of ten. I was stimulated by the events of the day before. The job was tailor made for me. Between my background in construction and sales, I was poised to meet my goal of becoming a millionaire. I had been living off the envelope of commission money from Sammy's hotels and it was getting very slim. I knew I had nothing to worry about. Unlike my mother, my pretend father always took care of me in the end. I was about to make him even happier, since there were already a few new customers waiting when I pulled up to the office.

Stephan and I negotiated many deals that day. The job required us to go back and forth to the park and look at more trade-ins and visit more customers. Though we did not close every last one, the promise of the next day's closings was huge. Without any time for lunch, and before I could take a breath, it was already eight o'clock at night. I was still at the lot and we were still busy, but the best part was letting Jerry know how good we were doing. I couldn't resist calling – even though there were still a few customers milling about. Before I could revel in boasting of our hard work and tell Jerry about all the deals we had pending, he asked if I had sold anything and if there was any money for the bank. That was no fun! I expected a nice little pat on the head. I told him that I would work harder the next day but I still had more things to do that night before I closed down.

Stephan and I were both starving and exhausted. I invited him to dinner again across the street. It's a good thing Jerry had given me that envelope with money because that's all I had left to my name and Stephan had even less. I was afraid to come right out and ask Jerry for money. It seemed like he would rather give it in one generous-looking lump sum of a commission. The envelope was so slim I feared I might have to beg.

Stephan and I ate dinner with our heads barely above the table. I left straight away after dinner.

I rushed home. I was dying to find out what had happened after I left the Monkey Business, so I called Lynn. She told me that Donna and Gary had gone to Bimini together and that Gary had invited Donna to Washington to meet him at his townhouse. I was a little shocked; not that Donna would take off with a rich man, but that he could be so cavalier about it. It prompted the next question, "Is he still running for president?"

We both laughed at the question and then she invited me to go out again that night. I regretfully turned her down. I couldn't move. My arm was pulsating with pain and I was exhausted. I hadn't been wearing my wires because I didn't want to scare the customers. I had been warned by my doctor that going too long without them would leave me handicapped, so I wired up and went straight to bed.

The next morning I stopped to get fuel and when I went inside to pay I saw Donna's face all over the National Enquirer. She was coming out of Gary's townhouse. I bought the tabloid fearing that somehow my photo would be in there, too. There were all kinds of photos from the night on the Monkey Business. Luckily, I was not in any of them. I thought about calling Lynn to see if Donna was okay, but got distracted by the many customers waiting for me at the office.

The following day I got a call from a mutual friend of Lynn's and Donna's and mine. He told me that it was Lynn who tipped off the Miami Herald reporter about Donna and sold the whole story for a million dollars and left town. That was more shocking to me than anything Donna had done. That evening Gary Hart resigned from the presidential election.

Chapter 22
TWO NEW LOVES

The next several months were filled with a barrage of Canadian customers and big commissions for Stephan. I worked my ass off day and night setting up the deals, overseeing deliveries, creating contracts and sweet talking Stephan into translating in French. Jerry's set up was that the closer would get the commission, which came to about fifteen hundred a week. Since I didn't technically close any of the deals I waited patiently for Jerry to pay me. I was in awe of Jerry so I did not make demands on the most powerful man I knew.

After about three months of steady sales, I had not yet been paid a thing. It got so bad that when my final notice on my electric bill came I had to do something. Since I had signing privileges on the company checkbook, I made one out for three hundred dollars to my electric company. To be forthright I sent Jerry a copy of the check. This did not go well with him. He flipped out and accused me of stealing. Stealing? I lost my patience and flipped out right back at him. I told him that I was broke and reminded him that he had not paid me anything in almost four months. After much deliberation, he came back with a plan that I was to receive five hundred dollars per week in salary and a percentage of the net profits at the end of the year. I was happy to get anything this influential man would choose to bestow upon me. Pleased with myself, I went home to catch up on all my other bills.

Working with Stephan for hours on end amplified our relationship. We would celebrate every sale and worry when one was falling out. Close quarters made for close feelings and the friendship grew.

One night after work we stepped it up a notch, all because I went to watch him race his motorcycle. The correct male/female ingredients were intermingling. He looked hot and sexy doing his dangerous sport and I did my part by cheering him on. He won the race and we celebrated over dinner and wine. When he stepped into my apartment, still dressed in his sexy racing clothes with the dirt of the conquest all over him, threw me against the wall and laid an amazing kiss on me, I was appropriately beguiled. I hadn't expected such passion from the young trailer-living boy. And when he dragged me into my favorite stress-release rain box to wash off all the dirt from the track, I was a pool of lust. We fooled around till morning. What an interesting night.

That morning we drove to work together. Stephan was telling me how much he liked me and how we were going to have a great relationship. He promised he was going to make me so happy. I was not sure that was what I was looking for, but decided to keep listening for a while.

Eight months had gone by and my financial position had not changed while Stephan's and Jerry's bank accounts were growing. I remained patient, as I knew Jerry would reward me in the end.

Stephan moved in soon after the racetrack affair. For some reason, I felt obligated to care for him. Even though he was getting paid well I did not charge him rent or utilities or anything. He rather loved his cushy situation. Meanwhile, I was barely covering my ass.

Jerry was becoming tyrannical. He would call often and ask how much we had made and how much I had deposited into his bank account. He didn't approve of my relationship with Stephan, but he did like the idea that the happier I kept Stephan, the more he would close on those cute little houses.

Whenever I approached Jerry about a commission, he refused. He was adamant that I stay on salary. I never understood this and I never questioned it. I had no reason not to trust him. In fact, he was about the only person I *could* count on. I noted the large amount of money he was earning from this little company. Every time Jerry and I would speak about it, he called it *our* company. That was magic to my ears. Off I would go to work harder for *our* company. And even though I was still far from making my millions, I was building equity.

A year had gone by and I began feeling somewhat discontented. We were selling the little houses at a fairly steady rate, I was still on salary with a few little bonuses thrown my way, and Stephan was getting on my last nerve. That's what happens when you foolishly pay for everything while your young "boy" friend selfishly bankrolls his money. He rarely even bought me so much as lunch. I wanted him out.

It wasn't an easy task as he was in love with me. It was pure torture to work with him all day long and then go home to more of the same. I finally understood why you should never date people at work. You practically had to hit me over the head with a hammer, but in the end I got it. Do not mix business with pleasure because it takes ALL the pleasure out of *everything*. After another three months of suffering, he moved back to the office trailer and then back to Canada.

Au revoir.

I hired a new salesman.

In the middle of all the Stephan chaos, I had received a notice from the owner of my townhouse that he was selling to his father-in-law and needed me to move. I had very little bonus money saved up so I tried to crunch numbers in order to buy my own piece of real estate instead of throwing it away on rent. Jerry the mentor agreed with my line of thinking. Within two days I found the perfect townhouse belonging to two lesbians that were splitting up. Thanks to Jerry's clever mind and gracious help, I was able to buy it with only fifteen hundred dollars down. I became the proud owner of my own place at the age of twenty-four.

One fortuitous day I ran into an old friend I knew from Studio 54. Her name was Tina and in the course of our conversation she mentioned that she had her horse, Scamp, with her just down the street from my office. When Tina invited me to her place to ride, I was both terrified and ecstatic. My adoration for horses took over my being. I had not been on one of the magnificent animals since I was brutally mangled all those years before. My life experience to that point had been all about "getting back on the horse". When people like Billy, Dan the Probation Man, my mother or José threw me, I got right back to my life. I didn't let anything get in the way of starting fresh with a positive and hopeful attitude. Now I was being challenged to physically get back on the horse. I wasn't about to let my fear get in my way now.

For the following months I would tell the salesmen at work that I was visiting our customers during my lunch break when I was going to Tina's to ride Scamp.

On my first drive to the ranch my palms started sweating - just like the first time I walked back into Apartment Five. Good thing I naturally tended to focus on the impending outcome rather than the original tragedy. I think that was my true gift in life. From the time my mother threw me in the deep end, I had set my sights on the edge of the pool. It seemed a harsh lesson at the time, but somehow I interpreted surviving that one disturbing act as a positive. And though I could not trust others - mother, father, brother, friends, or even the recipient of my kindness - I could always trust in *myself*. No matter what happened in my life, I knew on a cellular level that I would eventually find the edge of the pool. I was unstoppable.

I got right back on the horse and let him bring wind to my hair and love to my heart. That was the feeling I had been longing for. That was the main reason I strived to become a millionaire. I wanted to own horses - lots of them. Getting atop of Scamp made it all come flooding back. This is where I belonged. And this was the impetus I needed to achieve my goal.

Tina was an accomplished rider who had received many awards as a hunter-jumper. I had never had a formal lesson in my life. I just had natural talent. I jumped at the chance when she offered to give me lessons.

After several months, Tina was able to break me of bad riding habits and taught me some great ways to get the most out of my jumps. Every day I looked forward to the moment I could get back on Scamp. He and I became best friends and my spirit was back to being light and happy. It was like I was eleven again. Then Tina made me an offer I could not refuse; she told me if I would pay Scamp's board I could have him. I was overjoyed. I wasn't sure how I was going find the time to muck out his stall or get him food, but I accepted anyway knowing that if I could pull it off at age eleven, I'd figure out a way.

Larry, the new salesman, was not nearly as good as either Stephan or me. I hatched this clever plan that benefited everyone including Scamp. I took over selling and closing most of the little houses, but made Larry agree to give me half on the ones I had been responsible for. Since Jerry would not budge on the status of my salary versus commission, we kept it our little secret. I sold my little ass off for Larry and kept half for myself. Between that and knowing I was paying a mortgage and not rent and building equity in "our" business, things were looking better. The millions were getting closer.

Tina and I became good riding buddies. She had gotten married to a blacksmith from the racetrack, and he had a friend named Donnie he wanted to fix me up with. They prepped me by letting me know that my future date owned racehorses - my dream come true - and was also a retired car dealer. We even had business in common.

I wanted to share my excitement about my up and coming date with Jerry. He was delighted for me. When I asked him if I could borrow the limo and driver - one of the perks of working with Jerry - he enthusiastically agreed. It was set up for Saturday night when I would pick up Tina, her husband and Donnie and go Joe's Stone Crabs - one of my favorite places.

Finally, date night arrived. I put on one of my best outfits. My wires and scars were now something of the past and I looked and felt hot that night. The driver came and we headed to Tina's. Tina's husband had been telling me about how Donnie had retired very young and that he had a string of horses. I was just hoping he was good looking. I hate to be so shallow, but looks were just as important to me as money. Actually, money was even second.

We pulled up; I was praying everything would be as good as had been promised. He came around the corner and I saw this handsome, six-foot, well-built man. He looked me square in the eye with his beautiful deep blue eyes and introduced himself as my future husband. With that said, I was sold. He did not let go of my hand and we drove off to Joe's Stone Crabs.

Chapter 23
BIG CHANGES

Donnie and I became a hot item. We saw each other every night after that first date. We had elaborate dinners and romantic evenings. He was attentive and complementary and debonair. I was charmed. I loved the distraction a new lover can have on a hard working girl. After a long twelve-hour day, I looked forward to Donnie's loving. We had so much in common. We both loved horses. Finally, here was someone I could relate to.

The first red flag presented itself early on, but I wasn't in the mood to notice. I had no other social life other than my new riding lessons, so having a regular boyfriend in the picture, a fellow horse enthusiast, was very comfortable. The only problem was that he never paid for anything. He would spend five hundred dollars on an amazing dinner, but when the check came he would disappear or tell me to put it on my credit card and promise to repay me. He would often invite his racetrack buddies to dinner with us and he liked to throw money around like it was growing on trees. He had such good excuses about why he didn't have money on him to pay for the night's extravagance, but he always seemed to have it for himself. I had to chase him to pay me back.

Several months went by and we were seeing each other even more, though we didn't live together. He had his own place with his older son. I liked the arrangement because when we would get in a little fight, he'd go off to his own place to pout and I would get a good night's sleep.

Once in a while he just stayed or passed out. He was quite a heavy drinker. By seven p.m. he would start in with the rum and cokes or a six-pack of beer. He'd be passed out by eleven and would be woken by my screams every night around three. Donnie showed concern for the first several days, then it became routine; I'd scream just in time for him to get up and head to the track to take care of the racehorses.

Our relationship soured a bit after a while, but neither of us broke it off. Maybe I was just too busy to formulate a plan. I was selling my ass off twelve hours a day, seven days a week in between putting up with Jerry's demands about putting more money in the bank. I was responsible for that whole operation and it was never enough for Jerry. By the time I would get home Donnie would be waiting for me already drunk. He was possessive and could get mean-spirited and would torture me by asking about the men I might have talked to, questioning what I had done all day.

The one good thing during this phase of my life was that Donnie had famous racehorses. They were always winning and people would constantly call for betting tips. I loved the horses and the track and the whole scene. Unless Donnie got really plastered, we had a lot of good experiences going to the track. I loved his horses and I would go talk to them whenever I could. Donnie was the first person that not only tolerated but truly understood my passion for horses. He felt the same way. He would come watch me ride and I would fall in love with him all over again. That appreciation was the basis of our love.

Donnie asked me out to a romantic dinner on Valentine's Day. It was really sweet of him, even if I had to put it on my credit card. We were having a little toast when he asked me to marry him.

I considered it for a minute and started to see how it might be a good thing for me. We had enough in common. I thought maybe if we married he might not drink as much. I accepted his proposal. I expected him to romantically put a ring on my finger, but he said he had ordered it and it was coming soon.

Donnie and I were excited to tell our families. He called his family right away. Donnie had two older sons; one that lived with him and the other was in the navy. They were both very happy for their father.

The first person I wanted to call was my mother. Don't ask me why. She never had a good thing to say, but damn it, we do need our mother's approval. I was nervous. It had nearly been nearly two years since I had spoken to either my mother or my brother. We were not on good terms. The last time I heard her voice she was berating me for losing Ivan's money. Apparently he was giving her a hard time about it. Ivan never called me for anything, so he took it out on her. I was nervous, but I wanted to at least tell my own mom that her only daughter was getting married. It was a time for celebration, but how could I break the ice with this happy news? She answered. I hesitated for a moment. I almost hung up. I started with hello and asked how she was. She answered with very short and firm words.

"Mom, guess what? I'm getting married," I said with hope.

Silence.

"Mom?"

A few seconds later she replied, "SO WHAT DO YOU WANT *ME* TO DO ABOUT IT?"

I was overwhelmed with disappointment and answered meekly, "Nothing. Sorry to bother you." I hung up. I didn't feel like calling anyone else.

After I got to the office the next day I wanted to tell Jerry, but decided to wait until I had some good news about the business first and then dial his number. That was the best way to break any news.

Finally, by seven p.m., I had some sales cooking so I called. He was happy about the potential sales and didn't have much to say about my getting married. He just told me not to rush.

Over the next several months I planned a large wedding. I picked out the most beautiful dress and put a deposit on it. Since I didn't have a father to give me away, I asked Jerry. He was delighted and that made me feel good. As often as I knew my mother would disappoint me, I also knew Jerry would support me. I still had to pay for the whole thing, but that was okay. I told myself that I would just work a little harder so Jerry and Donnie would be proud. The two of them became racetrack buddies.

Months went by and I continued to work feverishly running the operation. We gained three sales people, a secretary and a few service techs. One day I got a call from Ivan. It was so strange to hear from him. He said he had just lost his job as a valet on the beach because the hotel had been sold, and he wanted to know if I had a job for him. The fact that he was family and had lent me money (involuntarily) to buy the apartments, I wanted to help him in any way I could. I quickly gave him the details of the salesman job and told him to come right away. We never discussed anything of the past or my mother; he just wanted a job. I began to train him in the world of selling little houses on wheels.

I eventually moved Scamp to the pasture board and bought a two-year-old off the track. I found a new trainer to coach me to further my riding skills. I was still doing the same thing; lying to the sales people, Jerry, and now Ivan, as to my whereabouts. Riding and showing horses was a vital part of my spiritual life. It was the one way I felt both stimulated and safe at the same time. In the midst of pressures of work, not knowing if I was coming home to a drunken fiancé, trying to accommodate my brother, hoping Jerry would someday recognize my talents, and trying to sleep a full night without screaming, I needed to ride in order to feed my soul. It was imperative to my well-being that I play hooky on my lunch hour and get on my beloved horse. If Jerry called everyone was instructed to tell him I was outside with a customer or at one of the mobile home parks. God forbid I have a few minutes of daylight to myself.

One night I arrived home and Donnie was waiting, already drunk. We started fighting. I just told him to go home and we would talk tomorrow. He wasn't finished, though. His temper wanted to express itself, but I dismissed him and went upstairs. He followed me into the bedroom and the next thing I remember was the feeling of his hands around my throat. He was drunk and yelling but all I could see was José. I was waiting for a knife to come out. Within a few seconds, he snapped back to reality and started apologizing. I asked him to leave before someone got hurt so he did.

The next day he was very apologetic. I didn't want to have anything more to do with him. After several months of begging and filling me with words of contrition and promises to change, I usually caved. I spent such a large portion of my day at work and there was hardly any time for starting over and dating. Donnie was a convenient partner. Besides, I missed the racehorses.

He was on great behavior after that. We got along quite well and he only fell into that drunken behavior infrequently. We didn't argue very often and we actually enjoyed each other's company. Two months later I found out I was pregnant. I was not happy about this news. I had just bought another new horse and I was looking forward to showing him. This situation was messing up my plans.

I wasn't sure what to do. This was different from my first pregnancy. This time I was older and living on my own and had a fiancé. I assumed Donnie would be as inconvenienced as I was, but when I told him he was genuinely ecstatic. By the end of the evening, he was picking out girls names. I dropped any plans of aborting it. Once I accepted that a little soul was working its way in to be a part of my life, a little miracle happened and I began to fall in love with the baby.

I wasn't sure what Jerry's reaction would be. He was the closest parental type in my life and his opinion mattered a lot. We went to a late lunch one afternoon to talk about several business-related matters. After pleasing him with my reports and suggestions, I got the nerve to tell him.

"Well, Jerry, I'm pregnant."

He waited a second, just like a father might do. "Are you getting married?"

"I don't think so. I don't want to get married just because of the pregnancy. If it was meant to be, we would already be married," I reported matter-of-factly. I was ambivalent, to tell the truth. Donnie had been cool over the past few months, but I did not forget that one hideous José moment.

It wasn't long before Donnie and I were back to fighting over money. He was still making me pay for everything and he would run my credit cards into the ground. I realize that no one could force another to pay for nice dinners, so maybe his behavior would be better described as manipulative. I have to admit that I did not stand strong enough. The more he used me to support his gambling habit, the more I pulled away. Finally, I stopped seeing him altogether. Months went by and my baby kept on growing.

When Hurricane Andrew hit Miami I was prepared to do emergency housing for people who lost their houses. I made Jerry millions over the next few months. I got a small sales commission but it was good. We made so much money we bought a brand new, state-of-the-art dealership with six service bays and over three acres of

RVs. Because of my previous knowledge of real estate, I did a thorough job of due diligence to prepare for the closing. Though Jerry never gave me credit for all I accomplished for him, he wore his pride on his face.

It became time for me to start my Lamaze classes as the baby was due in six weeks. I had so much on my plate I worried that I would not be ready. Soon after we had last parted, Donnie began his pattern of begging me to come back. The promises started up again and he was back on good behavior. I decided he could come with me to the classes since this was his baby, too. I would see him for my class two nights a week, and during the day I was trying to get everything done so we could close on our new dealership. All the while the little being was twisting and kicking, reminding me of the truly big event to come.

In my ninth month, Donnie pleaded with me to give the baby his last name, but I wasn't sure I wanted my child to have a different last name than mine. I hesitated.

On September twenty-seventh, 1993 Donnie called me at the office. I was hot and fat and incredibly miserable. He wanted to come by and pick me up and get married right then. So, in a weak moment, I grabbed Ivan to be my witness and the three of us went to the courthouse. Donnie and I got our license, stood before a judge and we were married. I wanted to go back to work to oversee the paperwork for the new acquisition, but both Donnie and Ivan agreed I should take the rest of the afternoon off since it was my wedding day.

By coincidence, the following day I got a call from my mother. She sounded very energetic and perky. For a split second I thought maybe Ivan had told her about my marriage and she was calling to congratulate me. Instead she told me in an unusually animated voice that she had gone to her class reunion back in Pennsylvania and had run into her high school sweetheart. They were enamored with each other, so much so that he instantly asked her to marry him. He had one condition before he would slip the ring on her finger; he wanted to meet her children. She was calling because she wanted Ivan and me to meet her and her beau for dinner that night. I wanted to say, "WHAT DO YOU WANT *ME* TO DO ABOUT IT?" But I didn't.

I hate to keep score, but I had not talked to my mother in years, except for the announcement of my betrothal when she slapped me down. Now she called because her potential husband won't participate in their union unless he meets me? She did not waste any time on questions about how I was, what my life was like, maybe saying, "Let's let bygones be bygones" - no. She couldn't have cared less. When she was not surprised at my belly when I showed up with Donnie, I realized that Ivan had been keeping her up-to-date.

Frank was the lucky man's name. He was very nice and was crazy about her. They were planning to go to the courthouse the next day. It was sweet how Frank wanted Ivan's and my approval. I asked the happy couple if they would like to go on a trip to Australia and Hawaii - all expenses paid. I had won it for being the number-one dealer for the year, but with my little one ready to appear in this world at any minute, I could not take advantage of the gift. In my ever-pleasing attempt to get Betty to love me, I offered it up. Nice honeymoon gift. They were thrilled. Bon Voyage, Mother and Stepfather.

It's a good thing I gave the trip away because one week later I went into intense labor. Fourteen hours of hard work - something I was used to, but the newborn was not. I went into cardiac arrest after they gave me the epidural, so an emergency C-section had to be done. After monitoring him and cleaning him up, the nurse put little baby Jarryd into my arms. I have heard of how that magical moment forever bonds a mother to her child, but I was simply terrified. I wanted instructions with this little guy. And what about a warranty? I had no maternal instincts. I hoped to get some soon. After four days in the hospital, I went home with my new son and husband. Two days later I was back at work with a hired twenty-four hour a day nanny. I could only hope and pray she would be to Jarryd what Lulu was to me.

I could barely walk with my stitches covering my stomach again. As I pulled up to the new dealership, there was a customer already waiting for me. He wanted to see all the units. After showing four, I was walking with pain and effort. He noticed and asked if I was okay. I smiled a pasty smile and told him I had just had a C-section. I had to admit that I could not walk any further. He felt so bad he bought the most expensive little house I had.

Donnie finally decided to sell his house and live with me because it was closer to the track. I begged him to let me sell mine and put the money together to buy a little farm. He put me off. His house sold within a month and he moved in with me. After three months of me paying all the bills, I decided to sell my house. Then we would be forced to do something. I sold it in three days... with a very nice profit. Homeless, I quickly started real estate shopping. Every time I picked out a suitable house I would have to wait for Donnie's approval and then it would get sold before he decided.

I was relieved when we settled on a cute four-bedroom place. There was plenty of room for Baby Jarryd, his nanny, Donnie's son and us. It was not perfect, but it had a lot of potential. It had a pool, and a barn. Once my horses were in the yard, life would be great.

Donnie agreed that we would both put in one hundred thousand - he from the money earned on his previous house. We would use my good credit for a loan.

When it came time for the closing, Donnie never came up with any money. This just served to further prove marrying him was a mistake, but it was done and I needed to move forward. I went back to my mentor for ideas. Jerry and I figured out a way to get into the house with next to no cash. The deal included a promise of me paying them with the profit I made when I closed on my condo. Thankfully it all worked out and we all moved in.

Though Donnie had slept over many times, we had never officially lived together. Boy, what a surprise - and not of the fun kind. I packed a lot into my day beginning with time with the baby, still working twelve hours a day, sneaking out to ride and hauling back to the office in time to call Jerry so he would know that I had called from work. He always wanted a full report. He was strict about it and pressured me about how much money I was going to deposit into the bank every single day. While trying to balance all that, I kept getting interrupted by my irritating husband complaining about things like what the nanny did with the dirty dishes. When I finally got off work, I would come home to an inebriated, belligerent spouse who accused me of fooling around with my horse trainer or anyone else I happened to talk to.

His deep anger was fueled by hours of boredom and Budweiser. He got worse as time went on. He would push me around the house. He tore all the cabinets off the walls. As he punched holes in our walls, he'd say that he wished it was my face. Between Jerry never being satisfied with what I did no matter how hard I worked and Donnie spinning me around like a helicopter, I found myself in a nightmare all over again. I didn't know which way was up.

This intolerable existence went on for about nine months. One dreary day, Donnie called me at the office and started screaming that the nanny had eaten his leftover steak. He demanded to know what I was going to do about it. Obviously intoxicated, he repeated the steak incident over and over again. On the other line Jerry wanted to know about business because there wasn't enough money for payroll. I took a deep breath, ignored my insane husband, and tended to Jerry's call. I promised him that business was fine, explained how it all worked and that we would be able to meet payroll. I was still only getting my $500 per week and I hoped he wasn't going to cut my pay.

Anticipating a big fight because I had hung up on him, I was relieved to see Donnie wasn't home when I arrived. Actually, I was rather happy. The nanny took the night off and Jarryd and I cuddled in the rocking chair in front of the TV.

All of a sudden, I heard and felt a big crash. Donnie drove through the front door and tried to run us over. With Jarryd in my arms as tight as I could hold him, we ran for cover, locked ourselves in the bathroom and called the police. Donnie was trying to knock the door down but the police got there in time. They asked him to leave. That's it. A polite "Sir, we're gonna have to ask you to leave the premises." That's all. They couldn't arrest him since there was not a mark on me. Donnie grabbed some things and left. I lay awake all night thinking he was coming back for me.

The next morning, walking out of what used to be the front door, I felt like I lost two hundred pounds: - named Donnie. This was like the first day of my new life again. No matter what kind of financial mess I was in, just like before, it was better than the alternative.

When I got to the office with Jarryd and the nanny in tow as usual, I knew I had to deal with Jerry's angst about the cash flow. Even though I was selling a lot of trailers, Jerry would always say the expenses were too high (I never saw the fixed cost). After telling him about my night, he expressed concern but quickly changed the subject to his bank account. I was getting the feeling that the father-daughter relationship was somehow compromised by the challenges of money.

When Jarryd, the nanny and I got back home, I noticed Donnie had come for his things. He took everything - all the furniture from the kitchen to our bedroom, even the barbeque grill - everything but Jarryd's crib. There I was once again sleeping on the floor, but at least I was content.

For several days, my riding buddies showed their true friendship by taking care of me. They checked on us while the front of the house was being repaired; they brought food, chairs and a bed, kept me company and helped me with Jarryd while I took a riding lesson after work.

The Fourth of July was approaching and I wanted to thank my friends for their concern by having a small pool party after my riding lesson. Pablo, my trainer, suggested I leave my horse at his place for the night. It was close to my barn and since I was scheduled to take an early lesson the next day, I agreed. It was like I had created a little safety zone of riding buddies and Pablo. It felt good to be single again, especially with the connection with others who loved horses as much as I. That night we celebrated till one in the morning. I fell asleep feeling satisfied and appreciative. This fresh start was essential.

I woke to screams. This time they were not mine. It was my riding buddy Julie. She came back to tell me that there had been a fire at Pablo's barn. I couldn't believe my ears. Through her hysterics, I made out that twenty-one horses had been burned to death. I stood there horrified and - frozen for a moment. I tried to console Julie. Then I remembered I left my horse there. Julie told me she had perished, too. I looked out the window to my barn hoping maybe she had been mistaken.

I had to find out myself and maybe this was a horrible dream - or maybe Julie was wrong. I ran out to my barn carrying as much hope as I could, but her stall was empty. I threw on some clothes and we drove to Pablo's. It was impossible to get near, as fire engines, police and news reporters were everywhere. We stood at a distance hoping against odds that maybe our babies had gotten out in time.

I was sick to my stomach as I waited the three hours to get my proof. I had this eerie feeling that maybe Donnie had something to do with it. He hated me and he hated Pablo. Maybe the idea that I was having a party made him crazy. I knew he was capable of something as unspeakable as this.

When I went to my horse's blackened stall, all I could find were her four shoes. It was pure devastation. Tears were escaping, but it was the silent scream that was building within. In pure shock and disgust, I walked out only to find a camera and microphone shoved in my face. Wiping away my tears, I told the news reporter the very sad story about the twenty-one amazing animals that lost their lives.

I pulled myself together and headed to work before Jerry could suspect I had been out of the office all morning. I was told that Donnie had called. He must have heard about the fire. I called him back expecting his sympathy, but a smashed voice said with pure antagonism, "I saw you on the news. You looked awful. I'm embarrassed that I ever married you."

That was not even worth a response. I couldn't think of the fire without cringing with horror. I needed to keep busy. Jerry called right then. I told him what happened and he felt sorry for me, and then we went on to business. It was better to keep my mind busy.

Later that week, I filed for divorce.

Repeating my parent's crap, I began my journey to the courts to fight over child support and just like them; I ended up giving all my money to the lawyer.

One day I got a strange call from a girl who said that a friend of hers was an ex-girlfriend of Donnie's. She tried to trick me into believing it was her friend but I could tell she was talking about herself. She stated that if I gave her five thousand dollars she would tell me where Donnie had hidden all his money. I took in this information. I had always suspected that he had money hidden. Her offer was tempting. If I could get my hands on that bastard's cache, I could get the child support I needed and pay some of the debts he had left me. I was financially ruined by that time and was heading for bankruptcy.

I asked her to prove she was who she claimed to be. She started by telling me what kind of shampoo I used, the clothes I wore and the things I kept in drawers and the kind of sheets I had on my bed. It was very disconcerting. It turned out that girl had been having an affair with Donnie long before we were married and up until a week ago. She had been sleeping in my bed in the afternoon while I was hard at work. Whenever I was out of town she wore my clothes and drove my car. I didn't know if I should love her or hate her. I settled with her for two thousand and gave the info to my lawyer.

Within several weeks, we got a new hearing. Even with this new information, I was weary. I always won the hearings. The problem was that the judge never made Donnie follow through and pay. Then we would go to another hearing, I'd pay my lawyer, he would win, no one would pay up. This stupid pattern went on for years. At one point, the judge threw Donnie in jail for nonpayment of child support, and then released him three months later without paying. With all my newfound evidence and Donnie's hidden assets, I ended up settling for seventy dollars per week and he was allowed to keep all his millions. To this day he has not yet made the first payment.

Three years later business was doing very well. I had turned the company around from losing four hundred and fifty thousand to making over three million dollars - all for Jerry.

He was getting older and very cranky. He was never satisfied anymore. One day while walking around the lot, I was approached by the neighboring car dealership asking me if I wanted to sell the property. I thought about it. If we sold our lot, we could make a nice little profit, Jerry could give me my piece, and I could move to a new location. The more I thought it through, the more appealing it was. I called Jerry right away. He shared my enthusiasm. I asked how much he wanted and he said around 1.7 million. Well, that's a nice little profit since we paid one million, so I asked the neighbor for 2 million - and he agreed at 1.95 million.

Jerry was happy and advised me to turn the deal over to his lawyer and he would take care of it from there. He instructed me to find a new location. I hesitated for a moment, thinking I just screwed myself out of a company, but quickly reminded myself that Jerry will take care of me. I went looking for more land.

I couldn't have been more wrong. As soon as the deal was signed, Jerry called and wanted out of the business. He told me to close everything down, fire the employees and liquidate the inventory. "Jerry, what about our company? All the work I put into it for only five hundred a week for all these years. I assumed that the rest was actually being invested in our company," I reasoned.

"If you want to buy the business, you can give me three hundred and fifty thousand and that's the best I can do. It's a steal for 350K."

"For what? There isn't any land left."

Something was fishy. It didn't add up. We made arrangements to meet the next morning at his lawyer's office. I called Barry.

I couldn't shake my suspicions that something was off, so I brought a small recorder and put it in my pocket. Barry and I sat next to each other across from Jerry and his lawyer. Looking at Jerry I was filled with sadness. The man I loved and adored practically my whole adult life was now the enemy.

Jerry excused himself from the room and his lawyer began to talk. He opened with, "You know you owe the bank 350k dollars."

I did not know what he was talking about. It turned out Jerry was not paying his loans as he had agreed. His attorney then reported that if I didn't pay this phantom bill I supposedly owed, he would tell the bank I stole it and I would never be trusted in the RV business again.

Barry and I looked at each other with disbelief. I could not believe that the man who I thought was the only person in my life I could count on would stoop to extortion. Hurt beyond belief, we excused ourselves and said we would get back to them with our decision.

The first thing I did was go to the office and retrieve all the evidence that would prove without a doubt that I put all the money in the bank and didn't steal anything. The next piece of business was to talk to the employees to tell them we were moving and that I would pay them. I wasn't sure how, but I knew I would figure it out. The good thing was that I wasn't legally liable for anything - I just wanted to be moral.

I made a deal across the street to rent a parcel of land within the place that used to be owned by our competitor. Fortunately for me, he was closing shop. I then made a deal with the soon-to-be owner to rent some space to give me time to move. We had been at our place for six years and there was a lot of liquidation to be done.

Jerry and I later struck a deal for me to pay him 150K over a period of two years for the phone numbers, two old trucks and a bunch of discontinued parts. That's all that was left of the three million dollar company. He had been quietly selling off assets.

Four years later, I was debt-free and thriving. I was in my early forties, but I finally reached my goal of making my first million... all by myself. I knew I had it in me. I just had to get around all the obstacles. I am grateful for the persistence and fortitude - whether I received those qualities from my parents or was born with them, they kept me from giving up when many women might have.

It was disheartening and amazing to find out how much Jerry had been taking from the company. It explained a lot about the urgency of his daily calls. It also clarified why he had never been satisfied with my performance. My mentor, my father figure, was just as deviant as most of the other people who got in way of my success. That part was the most disappointing of all.

One week after I made my final payment to Jerry, I got a call from a friend of his saying Jerry was in the hospital dying of cancer. No matter how brokenhearted I was to know Jerry had been deceiving me, I still loved him like a father. I started to cry. I got in my car and drove as fast as I could to the hospital to see him. We had not spoken since the day we had made the deal. I wanted to forgive him. I didn't want him to suffer.

Arriving at his private room, I was greeted by his nasty lawyer. Jerry's eyes opened wide. He looked weak. He lifted his head and raised a thin arm and motioned for me to come close. Then he said, "Hi Gigi. Thank you for coming to see me."

His voice was raspy. "I never meant to hurt you, my daughter."

214

We both had tears in our eyes. And then he gave a wry smile and said, "I always knew you'd land on your feet."

He had been following my success and knew all about the new dealership I had bought and of all the dealerships I had put out of business. He told me he was proud of me and it wasn't all for nothing.

I visited him daily. We would talk about stuff just like we used to, but his condition was quickly deteriorating.

Jerry passed away with only his lawyer by his side.

Because of his Jewish faith, his lawyer made funeral arrangement to bury him immediately. I didn't find out for several days. I never got to say goodbye. I cried for the brilliance he had brought to my world, for the times he had stood by my side when I was recovering from my stab wounds, for letting my mother know it was not okay to treat me so badly and for being the father I never had. I forgave him, from the bottom of my heart, for his weaknesses.

After all the bumps and bruises and cuts that marked my journey, I knew what Jerry had meant when he said I would land on my feet. Or as my mother would call it, "Getting to the edge of the pool." Or as I would call it, "Getting right back on the horse."

It's better than the alternative.

I have now been in the RV business for twenty-one years. I've built an 18.7 million dollar company with three dealerships; I own twenty-four horses and I have the most amazing fourteen-year-old son ever. Some would say I don't deserve it.

But I do!